Migration and Human Security in South Asia

Editor

Pramod Jaiswal

ADROIT

Adroit Publishers

NEW DELHI • KATHMANDU

ISBN : 978-81-87393-62-7

2021

Published by
ADROIT PUBLISHERS 4675/21, Ganpati Bhawan, Ansari Road,
Daryaganj, New Delhi-110 002 Phone : 011-23266030
adroitpublishers@gmail.com

Typeset in Garamond Premier Pro by Arun, Akriti Graphic
Solution, Delhi-110081 E-mail: arun263923@gmail.com,
Ph: 9999414390

Dedicated

to

Aahana and Rayan

Contents

Preface

Migration and security has been widely studied in international relations and political science. Migration is often presented as a threat to national sovereignty, state security as well as to the economic, social and cultural well – being. On security, all of the attention has been on national security, terrorism, extremism and crime. Hence, there is an alternative concept, human security, which emphasizes that the government's responsibility is not only to protect the territorial security and sovereign integrity of the state, but also the freedom and rights of its citizens. Thus, the notion of human security provides an opportunity to broaden our understanding of the economic, social and political challenges associated with migration, from the place of origin, to transit, arrival and (re) settlement in a new location. South Asia homes about one fourth of the world's population, making it both the most populous and the most densely populated geographical region in the world. This region has witnessed mass migration as many of the countries have emerged through partition.

The book consists of 11 chapters by scholars from India, Nepal and US on different aspects of migration and human security of South Asia such as impact of remittance on livelihood of Dalits of Nepal, illegal migration of Assam and Bangladesh, impact of Climate change in migration, Rise of anti-immigrants sentiments in South Asia and internal migration in South Asia.

Dr Binodkumar Singh highlights the main features of migration in South Asia, impact and vulnerabilities of women migrants. He also discusses the migration policies of South Asia.

Dr Sriparna Pathak explores the history of migration across porous borders and examines how a mixture of languages leads to the shaping of identities.

Dr Prakash Upadhyay looks at the impact of remittance on the livelihood of Dalit community of Western Nepal.

Dr Catherine Borshuk and Dr M. Gail Hickey address diverse aspects of South Asian immigrant identity via the scholarship on family dynamics, inter-group relations, cross-cultural psychology and educational psychology to consider such issues as: a) the impact of cultural practices and belief systems on immigrants' acculturative experiences, b) and immigrant families' experiences with formal institutions such as the US educational system.

Kundan Mishra takes a critical look at the growing interest in internal migration and leverages the concept of human security to identify some of key concerns facing the research on internal migration. He addresses five dimensions of internal migration research in South Asia. First, he looks at the evolution of the interest in internal migration in South Asia and explores the links between economic development, socio-economic inequality, and the agricultural economy. Second, he critically examines the existing, and growing body of, research on internal migration in South Asia and identifies their research focus. Third, he elaborates on the need to study agency of migrants and the drawbacks of conceptualizing migration as an interaction between rural and urban economies. Fourth, he evaluates human security framework to conceptualize vulnerabilities of internal migrants through an example of seasonal migrants in India and Bangladesh. He concludes by identifying key areas of research for internal migration and the necessity of an interdisciplinary approach to understand its multifaceted complexities.

Dr Shahnawaz Mantoo argues that illegal migration is posing several threats, particularly to receiving countries because the issue has not been properly securitized neither there is a proper mechanism to deal with it. He further argues that India should formulate a proper and lucid mechanism to manage such issues with the cooperation of neighbours involved.

Prasanta Kumar Sahu addresses the issue of security in the light of developments that have taken place in the post-cold war scenario. He also attempts to explore and enlarge the field of securitization theory to incorporate human security within the ambit of security studies. He also attempts to understand the nature of securitization theory and address the issue of natural disaster as a non-traditional security concern.

Shikha Gautam highlights the factors behind migration and how illegal migration impacts the region. She argues that states should have proper agreements over the issues of migration and regional organization and states that anti- immigrant sentiments could be minimized through the facilitation of better livelihood conditions in the destination countries which would help the migrants to mix together with the original inhabitants.

Oindrila Datta Gupta explores the idea of security and examines the non-traditional security concerns. She examines how the cross border migration brings with it a baggage of chronic human security threats such as hunger, fear, diseases, environmental pressure, exploitation and others which often threatens the state and society. She delves into migration issue between India and Bangladesh as a fulcrum of diplomacy and conflict between the two and investigates its impact on India's socio-political-economic stability with rising ethnic conflicts and informalisation of economy.

Dr Aditi Paul examines the concept of migrations as an international phenomenon that has made movement of people a global issue. She argues that both as a regional and global process, migrations raise pertinent questions about sovereignty, security, identity, means of livelihood, development and private property. Migrations take place for a reason and there are several triggers that not only lead to movement of people but also have an influence on the types of people that migrate. Thereby, migration as a problem is complex. She states that the relationship that migrant people develop with the demography of the host state is most critical in the framing of the policies regarding migrants and their rights and freedom. While harmonization and respect for freedom of human beings is crucial, one must take note that it does affect decisions on citizenship, stateless person, displaced people and so on. She believes that there is still much to be done and the responses from states and international organizations are weak and hesitant because migrations challenge the internal and external security paradigms of a sovereign state. She posits that in the era of multiculturalism and globalization of economic chains, it is hard to not accept transnational movement of people and provide them with rights. She aims to expand the existing knowledge on migrations and highlight the key issues and assess its trends.

Priyanshi Chauhan attempts to comprehend the way in which the phenomenon of climate change induces migration by linking climate change with human displacement in Bangladesh. Different combinations of push and pull factors including the income of the individual access to resources and economic opportunities at home, and availability and demand of resources at the place of destination, wage structure of the destination and social linkages between the place of origin and destination has been explored. She also attempts to look at the socioeconomic changes that accompany the phenomenon of climate change migration in Bangladesh and analyses existing international legal framework and government policies to deal with the issue of climate migration.

As a last word, I would like to mention that the authors have sole responsibility for all errors/ omissions and take full responsibility for the work being original.

Dr. Pramod Jaiswal
Editor

Acknowledgements

South Asia homes about one fourth of the world's population, making it both the most populous and the most densely populated geographical region in the world. This region has witnessed mass migration as many of the countries have emerged through partition. Migration is often presented as a threat to national sovereignty, state security as well as to the economic, social and cultural well – being. On security, all of the attention has been on national security, terrorism, extremism and crime. Hence, there is an alternative concept, human security, which emphasizes that the government's responsibility is not only to protect the territorial security and sovereign integrity of the state, but also the freedom and rights of its citizens.

The book consists of 11 chapters by scholars from India, Nepal and US on different aspects of migration and human security of South Asia such as impact of remittance on livelihood of Dalits of Nepal, illegal migration of Assam and Bangladesh, impact of Climate change in migration, Rise of anti-immigrants sentiments in South Asia and internal migration in South Asia.

It is the outcome of the combined effort of the authors of various paper incorporated in the book along with my personal contribution as an editor. Here, we would like to thank all the authors Dr Binodkumar Singh, Dr Sriparna Pathak, Dr Prakash Upadhyay, Dr Catherine Borshuk, Dr M. Gail Hickey, Kundan Mishra, Dr Shahnawaz Mantoo, Prasanta Kumar Sahu, Shikha Gautam, Oindrila Datta Gupta, Dr Aditi Paul and Priyanshi Chauhan for their timely submission. I would also like to thank many other senior scholars and friends who helped me and guided me in finalising the draft of the book.

Last but not the least; I would like to thank the publisher Adroit Publishers for providing all help and support for publishing the book.

Contributors

1. **Aditi Paul (Dr.)**, holds Doctorate in Peace and Conflict Studies from the Nelson Mandela Center for Peace and Conflict Resolution, Jamia Millia Islamia, New Delhi.
2. **Binodkumar Singh (Dr.)**, Research Associate, Institute for Conflict Management, New Delhi.
3. **Catherine Borshuk (Dr.)**, Associate Professor, Department of Psychology and Director of Women and Gender Studies Program at Indiana University, Indiana.
4. **Kundan Mishra,** Doctoral Candidate, University of Massachusetts, Boston.
5. **M. Gail Hickey (Dr.)**, Professor, Department of Educational Studies and Director of the Scholarship of Service-Learning at Indiana University-Purdue University Fort Wayne, Indiana.
6. **Oindrila Datta Gupta,** Doctoral Candidate, Centre for International Politics, Organisation, Diplomacy and Disarmament (CIPOD), School of International Studies, Jawaharlal Nehru University, New Delhi.
7. **Prakash Upadhyay (Dr.)**, Associate Professor, Prithvi Narayan Campus, Tribhuvan University, Nepal
8. **Prasanta Kumar Sahu**, Doctoral Candidate, Centre for Russian and Central Asian Studies, School of International Studies, Jawaharlal Nehru University, New Delhi.
9. **Priyanshi Chauhan,** Doctoral Candidate, Centre of South Asian Studies, School of International Studies, Jawaharlal Nehru University, New Delhi.

10. **Shahnawaz Mantoo (Dr.)**, Assistant Professor, Centre for International Relations, Islamic University of Science and Technology, Jammu and Kashmir.
11. **Shikha Gautam**, Doctoral Candidate, Centre for European Studies, School of International Studies, Jawaharlal Nehru University, New Delhi.
12. **Sriparna Pathak (Dr.)**, Assistant Professor, Department of Political Science, Nowgong College, Assam.

Abbreviations

AAGSP	:	All Assam Gana Sangram Parishad
AASU	:	All Assam Students Union
ADB	:	Asian Development Bank
AIDS	:	Acquired Immunodeficiency Syndrome
ATTF	:	All Tripura Tiger Force
BCCSAP	:	Bangladesh Climate Change Strategy and Action Plan
BDRCS	:	Bangladesh Red Crescent Society
BMET	:	Bureau of Manpower, Employment and Training
BOESL	:	The Bangladesh Overseas Employment and Service Ltd.
BSF	:	Border Security Force
BTAD	:	Bodoland Territorial Autonomous District
CBS	:	Central Bureau of Statistics
CHT	:	Chittagong Hill Tracts
DHD	:	Dina Halim Daigah
DNA	:	Deoxyribonucleic Acid
GDP	:	Gross Domestic Product
HDR	:	Human Development Report
HIV	:	Human Immunodeficiency Virus
HUJI	:	Harkat-ul-Jihad al-Islami
HUM	:	Harkat-ul-Mujahideen
ICISS	:	International Commission on Intervention and State Sovereignty
IDMC	:	Internal Displacement Monitoring Center
IDPs	:	Internally Displaced Persons
ILAA	:	Islamic Liberation Army of Assam
ILO	:	International Labor Organization
IMDT	:	Illegal Migrant Determination by Tribunal Act
INF	:	Islamic National Front

IOM	:	International Organisation of Migration
IPCC	:	The United Nations Intergovernment Panel on Climate Change
IPSS	:	International Peace and Security Studies
IRF	:	Islamic Revolutionary Front
ISI	:	Inter Service Intelligence
ISS	:	Islamic Sevak Sangh
IUCN	:	International Union for Conservation of Nature
IURPI	:	Islamic United Reformation Protest of India
JEI BD	:	Jamat-e-Islami Bangladesh
KLO	:	Kamtapur Liberation Organization
MLA	:	Muslim Liberation Army
MP	:	Member of Parliament
MSCA	:	Muslim Security Council of Assam
MSF	:	Muslim Security Force
MTF	:	Muslim Tiger Force
MULFA	:	Muslim United Liberation Front of Assam
MULTA	:	Muslim Liberation Tiger of Assam
MVF	:	Muslim Volunteer Force
NAPA	:	National Adaptation Plan of Action
NASA	:	National Aeronautics and Space Administration
NDFB	:	National Democratic Front of Bodoland
NELM	:	New Economics of Labor Migration
NFEA	:	Nepal Association of Foreign Employment Agents
NGOs	:	Non-Governmental Organization
NLFT	:	National Liberation Front of Tripura
NRI	:	Non-resident Indians
NWFP	:	North-West Frontier Province
OECD	:	Organization for Economic Cooperation and Development
PoR	:	Proof of Residency
PRSP	:	Poverty Reduction Strategy Paper
SAARC	:	South Asian Association for Regional Cooperation
SAWF	:	South Asia Women's Fund
SLBFE	:	Sri Lanka Bureau of Foreign Employment
SSP	:	Sipah-i-Sahaba Pakistan
TB	:	Tuberculosis

UILA	:	United Islamic Liberation Army
UIRA	:	United Islamic Revolutionary Army
ULFA	:	United Liberation Front of Assam
ULFBV	:	United Liberation Front of Barak Valley
UMLFA	:	United Muslim Front of Assam
UNEP	:	United Nations Environment Programme
UNDP	:	United Nations Development Program
UNHCR	:	United Nations High Commission for Refugees
UNHDR	:	United Nations Human Development Report
UNHRC	:	United Nations Human Rights Commission
UNODC	:	United Nations Office on Drugs and Crime
VDC	:	Village Development Committee
VVF	:	Village Voluntary Forces
WHO	:	World Health Organization
ZRV	:	Zomi Revolutionary Volunteer

Chapter One

Migration and Gender in South Asia

Binodkumar Singh

Abstract

Economic and social inequalities and political conflicts have led to the movement of persons within each country and across the borders in South Asia. A growing number of women in South Asia are migrating in search of better livelihood opportunities to support their families. By doing so, they are becoming economic actors rather than dependent spouses and financially independent. The different experiences of female migrants, the different conditions under which they migrate, and their differential reception in the countries they migrate to have also now garnered increased attention. A significant new trend is the increasing number of female migrants, but these women are especially vulnerable to hardship, discrimination, and abuse. Moreover, as women are often not considered a value-neutral workforce but rather symbols of national dignity and pride, the government tends to have protective and restrictive emigration policies for them. The impacts of migration on women, both those migrating and those left behind, is also not yet adequately understood or addressed by national or international policies. Millions of women left behind at home are facing an overwhelming burden. Increasingly, the workload on women left behind is multiplied many-fold. Not only must the women do household work and child and elderly care, but also generate income usually by taking on their husbands' role in agriculture. This too without access to capital or credit, while negotiating existing agricultural services dominated by men, where the women have to overcome several cultural barriers.

Introduction

Migration is a process encompassing any kind of population movement regardless of length, composition, or cause, either across an international border or within a state. It includes the migration of refugees, displaced persons, uprooted people, and economic migrants. Large-scale movements of voluntary and forced migrants have uprooted millions of people worldwide. Correspondingly, there has been an increased amount of attention given in both scholarship as well as pedagogy to the complexities of these movements of people, caused by varied reasons ranging from economic opportunity, ethnic violence, to social and political persecution. Economic globalization and the end of the cold war have led to the steady rise in cross-border flows since 1990, when there were an estimated 120 million migrants. According to the International Organization of Migration (IOM), there were 244 million international migrants out of a global population of 7.3 billion in 2015 accounting 3.3 percent of the global population. 48 percent of international migrants are women (IOM 2017).

Sadly, a growing number of migrants are dying in anonymity, far from home. In 2015, international migration became increasingly unsafe. A record number of 5,400 migrants worldwide are estimated to have died in 2015 trying to cross borders. The IOM estimates that over the last two decades, more than 60,000 migrants have died trying to reach their destinations, and this only includes deaths for which there is some record. In many cases, the bodies are never found or identified. Identification is difficult for many reasons. Local authorities tasked with investigating these deaths are often severely under-resourced. As many migrants travel without documents, migrants have to be identified by other means, such as tissue samples that can be used for DNA testing. But this information needs to be matched with that of family members who may not be easy to find, and who may not have legal access to the territory where the body is found. Bodies that are not found immediately in remote regions of the world can quickly become decomposed, making identification especially difficult (IOM 2016).

Cross border migration poses a big challenge for many countries, both in terms of the magnitude and variety of migration patterns and processes. If appropriately managed, migration can greatly benefit the individual as well as his/her source and destination communities. In contrast, poorly managed migration can result in various social, cultural, and economic difficulties, including public health problems such as HIV/AIDS, TB, and malaria. Nevertheless, migration is a natural process during the socioeconomic transformation of a country and cannot be stopped without coercive measures, which is not feasible in a democracy (Behra 2011). In addition, there is evidence that a city's migrant population makes a significant contribution to its economy, catering to labor demands at lower cost. Migrants make a huge contribution to the economy and culture of their source/destination countries by filling labor-market needs in high-skill and low-skill segments of the market, rejuvenating populations, improving labor-market efficiency, promoting entrepreneurship, spurring urban renewal, and injecting dynamism and diversity into destination countries and societies (ILO 2010). Although migrants are exposed to new risks, migration in the first instance reduces vulnerability and contributes to a secure livelihood and to reduced risks of seasonality, harvest failure, and food shortage (Sharma, Saraswati Das and Sarna 2015).

Migration in South Asia

South Asia is emerging as a migration hub of the world, because the percentage of total South Asian migration to international migrant stock was 13.33 per cent in 2005, and increased to 15.13 per cent in 2015 (Rajan2017). In South Asia, there are two distinct diasporas – the old diaspora born out of the 'age of colonial capital' and the new diaspora, an outcome of the 'age of globalization'. While the former was dominated by indentured labor serving the British Empire, the latter was mainly due to demand in developed countries for skilled and professional workers. With globalization, capital has become more mobile than labor but labor mobility takes place with the existing restrictions as demanded for labor has been increasing in developed countries (Kelegama 2011). The largest migration in South Asia occurred in 1947, accompanying the partition of the sub-continent into two nations India and Pakistan on the basis of religion -on the basis of religious differences and anxieties about minoritization after independence. In the nine months between August 1947 and the spring of the following year, by unofficial counts, at least 18 million people - Hindus, Sikhs and Muslims - were forced to flee their homes and became refugees; at least a million were killed in communal violence. The scale and nature of violence that India's partition involved makes it one of the most violent events in the history of nation formation (French1997). For the purpose of making things simpler, Partha Ghosh, in keeping with the circumstances that have contributed to their decision to cross the borders and settle in a neighboring state divide them into eight categories:(i) Partition-related uncertainties (ii) Failure in nation-building (iii) Inter-ethnic conflict (iv) Open or virtually open borders (v) War-related qualms (vi) Development and environmental effects (vii) Statelessness or virtual statelessness and (viii) Intra-regional and extra-regional military interventions (Ghosh 2016)

Notably, migration from the countries of South Asia can be divided into migration to countries outside the region (inter-regional migration), and migration to other countries within the region (intra-regional migration).

Inter-regional Migration: Inter-regional migration has gained in importance and is now the dominant stream for all countries in the region, except Bhutan and Maldives. Inter-regional migration comprises both low-skilled migrants to the Middle East, South-East Asia and other regions, and a smaller proportion of high-skilled migrants, principally to North America, Europe and other countries of the Organization for Economic Cooperation and Development (OECD). India and Pakistan are the largest labor-sending countries in the region. Labor migration from South Asian countries is male dominated; Sri Lanka is the only country in South Asia which promotes female labour migration. But although the proportion of female migrant workers is low for the region, it has been increasing over the years.

Intra-regional Migration: Intra-regional migration comprises a major share of all migration in the region. The actual flows are likely to be even larger than the official figures due to the huge undocumented flows of both permanent and circular migration. The major migration corridors in the region are Bangladesh–India, Afghanistan–Pakistan, India–Pakistan and Nepal–India. Studies of the profile of intra-regional migrants, such as Nepalese or Bangladeshi workers in India, show that they are employed primarily at the low end of the labor market, especially in the service sector. However, some migrants may acquire land or other assets over time. However, intra-regional migration in South Asia has shown a consistent decline since 1990. Such migration has become a source of concern for some of the region's countries, due to its socio-political, demographic, and economic impacts, and because of security concerns. The major issues related to cross-border migration in South Asia are irregular migration and human trafficking. Irregular and undocumented migration, particularly which is treated as "illegal", is an important issue in South Asian countries (Srivastava and Pandey 2017).

Main Features of South Asian Migration

The initial trigger for South Asian migration was the oil price boom in 1973 which created a large demand following massive construction projects. The subsequent decline in oil prices, and the end of the construction boom changed the character of migration to more service oriented sectors. The main features of South Asian Migration are as follows:

Temporary Migration of Labor: Most South Asian migration represents temporary migration on fixed term contracts. It is also a type of circular migration system which has stood the test of time over more than three decades, but it continues to be characterized by serious deficits in decent work including migrant rights. Permanent or settler migration from South Asia still takes place on a limited scale to Australia, New Zealand, the United Kingdom, and the United States, among others.

Predominance of Semi–skilled and Low–skilled Migrant Workers: Most migrant workers from South Asia to Middle East and other Asian destinations are low–skilled or semi–skilled, such as construction workers and female domestic workers. This phenomenon is a major cause of protection and vulnerability in both origin and destination countries.

Large Numbers of Migrants in Informal and Irregular Status: There is also incidence of "irregular migration" – commonly referred to as "illegal", "undocumented", or"clandestine" migration which can range from simple border crossings to organized trafficking and smuggling though there are no estimates of the numbers. The incidence of irregular migration is probably high in India and Pakistan, largely due to cross–border movements from Bangladesh into India and from Afghanistan into Pakistan, and continuing trafficking of women and children across the border from Bangladesh and Nepal into India.

Growing Importance of Female Migration: Another observed tendency has been the increasing share of female workers migrating on their own for overseas employment. The bulk of them migrate for low-wage occupations, such as domestic work. In South Asia, the share of female migration is high only in Sri Lanka, where currently about 50 per cent of migrants are female. Indian authorities however, do not provide any breakdown of emigration on the basis of gender.

A Thriving Recruitment Industry: The share of public employment services in overseas placements has fallen drastically in all countries, paving the way for a thriving industry of intermediaries in both origin and destination countries. Some are large firms with a good reputation, while many are unregistered small enterprises or individual sub agents. While the role of this industry in expanding opportunities for employment abroad has to be recognized, it is well documented that the recruitment industry has been responsible for high migration costs and various malpractices which seriously erode the development benefits of labour migration (Wickramasekara 2015).

Women Migration in South Asia

South Asia, including Bangladesh, India, Nepal, Pakistan and Sri Lanka, encompasses source, transit and destination areas for women who migrate for employment. Women migrate for employment within their home countries, within the region and to distant receiving countries including the Gulf, South East Asia and Europe. Women's increasing mobility across the region is catalyzed by aspirations for a better life as well as precipitated by increasing economic, political and environmental vulnerabilities. By shifting roles and emerging as mobile economic actors, South Asian women are challenging gender relations on the ground. Colliding with the reality of women's increasing mobility, however, patriarchal social practices that are anchored in protectionist laws and policies restrict women's ability to migrate for employment (SAWF 2016).

Migration from South Asian countries is largely male-dominated. Until the 1990s, only a small number of females migrated to overseas destinations, as doctors, nurses and teachers. Later, due to changes in the structure of the labour market, more women started to migrate, and this trend has increased over time. An increasing number of female migrants from South Asian countries are getting jobs in the newly emerging manufacturing sector, and as domestic workers in Gulf countries (Siddiqui 2008) However, most South Asian countries have imposed bans and age restrictions on female labor migration in order to protect female workers, particularly those working in households, from harassment and sexual exploitation. Such bans and restrictions have been imposed by the governments of Bangladesh, India, Nepal and Pakistan. However, the ban on female workers is thought to promote the illegal migration of women through informal channels (Ozaki 2012) Sri Lanka is the only country in South Asia which promotes female labor migration.

South Asia Migration 2017

	International migrants (thousands)	International migrants as percentage of total population	Females among international migrants (percentage)
Afghanistan	134	0.4	50.1
Bangladesh	1501	0.9	47.3
Bhutan	52	6.5	18.9
India	5189	0.4	48.8
Maldives	67	15.4	12.3
Nepal	503	1.7	69.4
Pakistan	3398	1.7	48.7
Sri Lanka	40	0.2	47.8

Source: International Migration Report 2017, Population Division, Department of Economic and Social Affairs, United Nations, New York, 2017.

However, gender-disaggregated data on female migrants are available for only a few countries such as Bangladesh, Nepal and Sri Lanka. These data and other studies suggest that the proportion of female labor migrants from the region remains low, but there is increasing feminization of labor migration from South Asia, largely associated with the migration of female workers from Sri Lanka and Bangladesh, as well as some undocumented migration from other countries. Female migrant labor in Sri Lanka represents almost half of the total migration abroad for employment, and it exceeded male labor migration in the 1990s and until recently (Wickramasekara 2010). The main destinations for female migrants from Sri Lanka and Bangladesh are Gulf countries and South-East Asian Countries, principally Malaysia and Singapore. Sri Lanka is the main sender of housemaids to Gulf countries and South-East Asian countries. Established social networks – friends, relatives and extended family members – have been found to play a major role in the increasing female migration from South Asian countries to these regions (Kabeer 2007).

Meanwhile, female migration in Nepal before the 1990s mainly took the form of associational migration, in which women accompanied their spouses, parents or relatives. The patriarchal culture, lack of reliable networks and unavailability of funds needed for female migration abroad hindered the emigration of independent women migrant workers for employment (Adhikari 2006). Political changes in Nepal during the 1990s, in which Nepal shifted from monarchy to democracy, had a great impact on the process of migration, both internal as well as international. During this period, failure of the agricultural economy and the resultant poverty forced many Nepalese women to migrate to India and other countries for employment (Bohra and Massey 2009). In spite of restrictions on women's migration to Gulf countries for work in the unorganized sector, large numbers of women workers from Nepal emigrate abroad through illegal channels, using border countries like India or Bangladesh as routes (NIDS 2010).

A range of factors compel women workers to migrate for employment. In addition to aspirations for better economic futures, significant push factors may include conflict related displacement, development driven displacement, agricultural decline, natural resource erosion, natural disasters and household-level economic distress. These migration push factors have different impacts upon women and their communities that are related to particular intersecting vulnerabilities. For instance, tribal communities from remote areas in Nepal were severely impacted by the earthquake but often outside the ambit of relief efforts. Women with disabilities reported facing heightened difficulties in migrating from affected areas and seeking employment to rebuild, their lives (SAWF 2016).

Until recently, migration studies have also tended to treat women's migration as primarily a consequence of male migration, and see women as merely accompanying or following husbands, fathers, or other related men (Boyd and Grieco 2003). However, a growing number of women in South Asia are migrating in search of better livelihood opportunities to support their families. By doing so, they are becoming economic factors rather than dependent spouses and financially independent (UN Women 2013). Across South Asia, restrictions on women's mobility prompt women to resort to irregular migration moving under the radar of formal migration processes. As their departure and work is undocumented they are more vulnerable to abuse, including precarious working conditions, low pay and exposure to violence and forced labor (UNHRC 2014).

Vulnerabilities of Women Migrants

As women are often not considered a value-neutral workforce but rather symbols of national dignity and pride, the government tends to have protective and restrictive emigration policies for them (Oishi 2002). But, women continue to be trafficked. The 2016 Global Report on Trafficking in Persons by United Nations

Office on Drugs and Crime (UNODC) released in December says women and girls make up 71 percent of human trafficking victims (UNODC 2016). Caste, social and community identity has significant bearing on migration patterns, pathways and the risks migrant women are willing to take. Migrant workers traveling in search of employment tend to be from some of the poorest, most marginalized castes and social groups in South Asia. As a result, they confront multiple and intersecting axes of discrimination and violence. These include, but are not limited to, discrimination on the basis of gender, caste, religious and tribal identity, marital status, sexual identity, class and disability (SAWF 2016).

Migrant women workers from socially and economically more vulnerable communities are also more likely to fall prey to exploitation by recruitment intermediaries, traffickers and employers. These women have comparatively fewer options for employment and may therefore be willing to take more significant risks to meet their personal and family needs. They may also have fewer networks and less information to guide them in their migration processes. Upon arriving in destination areas, migrant women from vulnerable communities largely work in low wage, unorganized and unprotected work. Women workers also typically find employment in the unorganized sector where their work is, undervalued, unpaid and invisible. Unprotected workers are usually engaged in employment without proof of employment either through company rolls or formal employment contracts. Undervaluation of women's work in the paid economy exacerbates the already precarious nature of women's employment (SAWF 2016).

Women who migrate for employment may face contradictory responses from their families and communities ranging from increased dependency to stigmatization. These responses are also reflected in state policies and practices. Increasing flows of remittances from women workers to rural and urban areas across the subcontinent are transforming women's lives and the lives of their families and communities. These contributions may affect subtle but important changes in the gender balance of power at the household and societal levels (Thinmothy and Sasikumar 2012). While some migrant women report having an increased say in family decision-making as a result of their economic contributions, others report that their contributions are quickly absorbed but largely unacknowledged. Despite their role fulfilling family responsibilities and state initiatives that promote migration for employment, women who migrate often face stigma in their families and communities. The impact of stigmatization upon women's ability to protect their rights can be profound. For instance, respondents reported that the stigma associated with migration causes many returnee migrants to hide their experience of migration and forego efforts to pursue accountability in cases of workplace and transit related abuse (SAWF 2016).

Studies on South Asian women left behind by migrant husbands have revealed intraregional variation in the impact of such separation on women's autonomy. For women, the outcomes of migration are multiple and contradictory. Women take on the responsibility for the house and childcare and can even lose their decision-making power if they stay with their in-law. If the men do not come home for harvest, women also have to take on the added agricultural work, or have to organize male support (Kaspar 2004). Moreover, women cannot continue receiving health care because they lack an accompanying person, they are hesitant to go alone, and they need to care for younger children at home. Thus, the rural migrant population is not only nutritionally insecure at present but is likely to be perpetually malnourished and vulnerable. Bias against women and girl children is also likely to be more conspicuous among people of rural origin, further affecting the nutrition outcome of females (Choudhary and Parthsarathy 2009).

Migration Policies in South Asia

Although an integrated approach towards migration both internal and international has begun to develop in some South Asian countries, international migration has received much greater attention and visibility in the region, and has been addressed through a range of policy measures. Most South Asian countries framed their existing legislation related to international migration after repealing the Emigration Act, 1922, which they were following due to their colonial heritage until the 1980s (Wickramasekara 2011). Following the oil price boom in the Gulf countries and subsequent demand for labor in the early 1970s, the migration of labor from South Asian countries to the Gulf increased sharply. Therefore, every South Asian country started to frame regulations related to international migration. Most formulated legislation on migration in the 1980s, and laws have since been amended from time to time to close loopholes. Some South Asian countries have framed fairly comprehensive policies addressing several aspects of international migration. Others are still evolving the appropriate institutional, regulatory and promotional framework for such migration (Srivastava and Pandey 2017).

In Sri Lanka, matters relating to migration and remittances are looked after by Ministry of Employment and Labour. It is supported by the Sri Lanka Bureau of Foreign Employment (SLBFE), which regulates overseas migration. The SLBFE Act No. 21, 1985, amended by Act No. 4, 1994, is applicable to all migrant workers (Thimothy and Sasikumar 2012). Sri Lanka enacted a National Labor Migration Policy in 2008. This policy focuses on enhancing the benefits of labor migration for migrant workers and their families, and working towards the fulfillment and protection of human and labor rights of all migrant workers. Apart from its National Labor Migration Policy, Sri Lanka has several other policies to promote and protect migrant workers, such as the Migration Health Policy, Technical and Vocational Training Policy for Migrant Workers, National Decent Work Policy, etc (IPSS 2013).

In Pakistan, the Emigration Ordinance, 1979 and the Emigration Rules, 1979 regulate emigration, overseas employment and recruiting agencies. Section 8 of the Emigration Ordinance manages the recruitment agencies and processes and protects workers' interests. The National Emigration Policy 2009 now protects overseas workers' interests. The Bureau of Emigration and Overseas Employment manages migration of private-sector workers, while the Overseas Employment Corporation manages public-sector migration (Khatri 2007). Pakistan introduced a National Emigration Policy in 2009 which acknowledges the lack of an information base on different aspects of emigration from Pakistan, such as the high cost involved in emigration, the need for upgrading skills and language proficiency to meet foreign demand, effective use of remittances, irregular emigration, protection of the rights of emigrants, lack of proper access to health and preventive services for HIV, and information before departure and after arrival of emigrants (Srivastava and Pandey 2017).

In India, the Emigration Act of 1983 replaced the British-era legislation of 1922. The focus of the new legislation has moved to a protective approach, with an emphasis on the welfare of the migrant population as well as the promotion of overseas employment. Despite limited capacity for redressing the grievances of a large number of migrant workers, the Government of India has taken certain steps to redress the grievances of migrant workers through public hearings in eight offices of Protectors of Emigrants in the country (Ministry of Labour

2002). The Emigration (Amendment) Bill, 2002 has proposed the establishment of a National Manpower Export Promotion Council, a tripartite organization comprising representatives of labor, management and the government. Taking into consideration, the importance of Indian migrants (non-resident Indians, NRIs) and their contribution to the GDP, the government of India created a new Ministry of Indian Overseas Affairs in early 2005. The Ministry has worked on strategies to develop welfare measures, introducing insurance scheme, issuing smart cards, and entering bilateral agreements with major labour receiving countries (Pong-Sul 2005).

In Nepal, the Foreign Employment Act, 1985 intends to regulate various aspects of labor migration ranging from the provision of recruiting agencies' license to the procedure of selecting workers. The Act also makes it mandatory for license holders to inform workers being sent abroad of employment issues including the geographical location, culture, labor laws, economic, political and social conditions of the destination countries. Moreover, the National Labor Policy, 1999 had some sections relating to foreign employment, but there was no effective policy to manage migration and remittances. Therefore, the Nepal Association of Foreign Employment Agents (NFEA) has a long-standing complaint that the 1999 policy is control-oriented and restrictive towards foreign employment. The Poverty Reduction Strategy Paper (PRSP) adopted by tripartite constituents in late 2003 suggested that the Government improve legal regulations and enhance its institutional capacity for managing migration. "Labor Migration Policy, 2005 proposed but not finalized within the Ministry of Labor and Transport Management, looks after the problems related to foreign employment and migrant workers as well as maximize the opportunities of foreign employment through the development of quality human resources (Ministry of Labour and Transport Management 2005). Further, Nepal's Foreign Employment Regulation 2008 takes a rights-based approach to migration. It opposes all gender discrimination and promotes women's migration (Thimothy and Sasikumar 2012).

In Bangladesh, the Overseas Employment Act, 2011 follows all rights based conventions of ILO and UN. The Ministry of Expatriates and Overseas Employment promotes overseas employment and the Bureau of Manpower, Employment and Training (BMET) protects the interest of emigrants and provides guidance and vocational skill training. The Bangladesh Overseas

Employment and Service Ltd. (BOESL) provides consulting services and recruiting agencies for overseas-employment seekers (Khatri 2007). Meanwhile, Afghanistan has no strong legislative framework to regulate labor migration. Regulations for Sending Afghan Workers Abroad 2005, deals more with obligations and less with workers' rights (Srivastava and Pandey 2017). Thus, despite the improvements in institutional structure and legislation related to emigration, initiatives relating to migrant workers from this region suffer from a lack of integration between the different ministries and departments which deal with the issues of migrant workers working abroad (Wickramasekara 2011).

Conclusion

Internal and international migration is an important part of the livelihood and employment strategy of individuals and households in South Asian countries. Both internal and international migrations lead to broadly similar consequences. Internal as well as international migrant workers, who are at lower end of the labor market, lack social security at the place of destination. They suffer from a range of vulnerabilities and deprivations. But, both types of migration have positive consequences for employment, poverty reduction and economic growth.

Most of the countries in this region have a range of policies to regulate and protect their emigrants, with varying degrees of coverage and effectiveness, but there are very few policies which focus on internal migrants. Given the common drivers and consequences of migration, its link with national development, and the need to respect the human rights of migrants, South Asian countries need an integrated rights-based approach towards different types of migration. This will enable them to forge a stronger link between migration, employment, growth and development and help them achieve national and global development targets.

Migration policies which always involve more than one nation should be based on interstate cooperation and dialogue. It should also involve broad based social dialogue involving employers, workers and civil society, all stakeholders. At the same time, it should be emphasized that labor migration is not a solution to problems of poverty and lack of development at home. Sound development policies would serve to create decent work opportunities at home, thereby facilitating migration by choice, and not by need in the long run, as highlighted by the Global Commission on International Migration.

The Governments in South Asia and its neighboring countries recognize the need for enhancing their institutional capacity and developing strategies to harness the positive impacts of out-migration and to achieve the goal of protecting migrant workers' rights. Rights of workers were important as rights of human beings, also necessitating a focus on gender dimensions. There is the need for inter-union cooperation between labor sending and labor receiving countries by way of networking, information-sharing and monitoring. There are various ways in which these can be done. First, trade unions intervention in some areas like pre-departure training programs and returnees' rehabilitation programs will be useful. A monitoring role by trade unions will be essential in regulating unscrupulous recruiting agencies. Networking between trade unions in labor-sending and labor-receiving countries can be a key to sharing migration information and providing effective services for migrant workers.

Governments tend to have protective and restrictive emigration policies for women, exposing them to further risks and deprivations in the process. These restrictive policies need to be reexamined and strive to: Promote safe migration for women in rural areas, including the prevention of trafficking in human beings, as well as the facilitation of rural women's access to reliable legal migration information, identity and travel documents, as well as migration services; Promote a better regulation of the migration of domestic and care workers in the countries of origin as well as promote protection mechanisms and adequate conditions of employment in the countries of destination; Promote gender-sensitive pre-departure orientation programmes for future migrants, including those engaged in transnational marriage migration; and Foster inter-State dialogue and enhance bilateral, regional, interregional and international cooperation to better regulate and protect women migrant workers and promotion of gender sensitive international migration policies.

References

Adhikari, J., 'Poverty, globalisation and gendered labour migration in Nepal,' in Arya S. and Roy, A. (eds), *Poverty, Gender and Migration: Women and Migration in Asia*, Sage Publications, New Delhi, 2006, pp. 87–106.

Behra, S., *Trans-border Identities: A study on the impact of Bangladeshi and Nepali Migration to India*, Policy Series, No. 1, ICRIER, May 2011.

Bohra, P. and Massey, D.S., *Processes of internal and international migration from Chitwan, Nepal,* International Migration Review, Vol. 43, No. 3, 2009, pp. 621–51.

Boyd, M. and Grieco, E., '*Women and migration: incorporating gender into international migration theory*', Special Issue, Migration Policy Institute, Washington, March 2003.

Choudhary, N., and Parthasarathy, D., *Is migration status a determinant of urban nutrition insecurity? Empirical evidence from Mumbai city, India*. Journal of Biosocial Science, Volume 41, Issue 5, September 2009, pp. 583-605.

French, Patrick, *Liberty or Death: India's Journey to Independence and Division*, Harper Collins Publishers, London 1997.

Ghosh, Partha S., *Migrants, Refugees and the Stateless in South Asia*, SAGE Publications, New Delhi, 2016, p. 2.

Institute of Policy Studies of Sri Lanka (IPSS), *Migration Profile – Sri Lanka*, Colombo, 2013.

International Labour Office (ILO), *International Labour Migration: A rights-based approach*, International Labour Office, Geneva, 2010.

International Organization for Migration (IOM), *Fatal Journeys: Identification and Tracing of Dead and Missing Migrants,* Global Migration Data Analysis Centre, 2016.

International Organization for Migration (IOM), *Migration Facts: International Migration*, Global Migration Data Analysis Centre, 2017.

Kabeer, N., Female Labour: Transnational Migration, Social Protection and Citizenship in the Asia Region, IDRC Working Paper No. 1, International Development Research Centre, Ottawa, 2007.

Kaspar, Heidi, *Impacts of International Labour Migration on Gender Relations: A Case Study of Kalabang, Nepal*, Master's Thesis, University of Zurich, 2004.

Kelegama, Saman, *Migration, Remittances and Development in South Asia*, SAGE Publications, New Delhi, 2011.

Khatri, S. K., *Labour Migration, Employment and Poverty Alleviation in South Asia*, South Asia Centre for Policy Studies, Kathmandu, 2007.

Ministry of Labour and Transport Management, *Labour Migration Policy*, 2005, Government of Nepal.

Ministry of Labour, *Annual Report 2001-2002*, Government of India.

Nepal Institute of Development Studies (NIDS), *Nepal Migration Year Book-2010*, Nepal Institute of Development Studies, Kathmandu, 2010.

Oishi, N., *Gender and Migration: An Integrative Approach, Working paper 49,* Center for Comparative Immigration Studies, University of California, November 2002.

Ozaki, M., *Worker Migration and Remittances in South Asia*, South Asia Working Paper Series No. 12, Asian Development Bank, Manila, 2012.

Pong-Sul, AHN, *Prospects and Challenges of Out-Migration from South Asia and its neighbouring countries*, Labour & Development, Vol 11, No.1, June 2005.

Rajan, S. Irudaya, 'South Asia-Gulf Migration Corridor', in S. Irudaya Rajan (ed.), *South Asia Migration Report 2017: Recruitment, Remittances and Reintegration*, Routledge, London, 2017.

Sharma,Vartika; Saraswati, Lopamudra Ray; Das, Susmita and Sarna, Avina, *Migration in South Asia: A Review*, Population Council, New Delhi, 2015.

Siddiqui, T, *Migration and Gender in Asia*, Paper No. 6, United Nations Economic and Social Commission for Asia and the Pacific, Bangkok, 2008.

South Asia Women's Fund (SAWF), *Gender and the right to mobility in South Asia*, Colombo, 2016.

Srivastava, Ravi and Pandey, Arvind Kumar, *Internal and International Migration in South Asia: Drivers, Interlinkage and Policy Issues*, UNESCO, New Delhi, 2017.

Thimonty, R. and Sasikumar, S.K., *Migration of women workers from South Asia to the Gulf*, V.V. Giri National Labour Institute, Noida, 2012.

UN Women, *South Asian Inter-Governmental Group calls for greater efforts to ensure safe migration of women workers*, Press-Release, 22 March , 2013.

United Nations Human Rights Council (UNHRC), *Report of the Special Rapporteur on the human rights of migrants, Francois Crépeau*, Twenty sixth session, Geneva, 3 April 2014.

United Nations Office on Drugs and Crime (UNODC), *Global Report on Trafficking in Persons 2016*, United Nations, New York, 2016.

Wickramasekara, Piyasiri, *International Migration and Employment in the Post-Reforms Economy of Sri Lanka*, International Migration Papers No. 107, International Labour Organization, Geneva, 2010.

Wickramasekara, Piyasiri, *Labour Migration in South Asia: A Review of Issues, Policies and Practices*, International Migration Papers No. 108, International Labour Organization, Geneva, 2011.

Wickramasekara, Piyasiri, *Mainstreaming Migration in Development Agendas: Assessment of South Asian countries*, Working Paper No. 02, Global Migration Policy Associates, Geneva, 2015.

Chapter Two

Migration in India: A Case Study of Kari Anglong in Assam

Sriparna Pathak

Abstract

As the world turns increasingly inward-looking and xenophobic, as seen in cases of the refugee crises in Europe or in the Rohingyas crisis in Asia, it becomes pertinent to analyse the contributions made by migration. It also becomes useful to look at how migrants change concepts of sovereignty and citizenship as they shuttle along in search of livelihoods among other concerns. India- a case of multiculturalism has several ethnicities coexisting and cohabiting and has multiple cases of how migration has historically led to the fulfillment of security and economic concerns. An interesting case becomes that of historical Nepalese migration to India- to Northeast India in particular wherein a plethora of languages and identities exist. For the purpose of this study, the district of Karbi Anglong has been taken as it is the largest district in Assam- the largest state of Northeast India. The paper begins with a history of migration across porous borders to how a mixture of languages leads to the shaping of identities; yet at the same time keeping the original linguistic identity intact. Sources for the study include primary as well as secondary sources.

Introduction

In 2016, the International Crisis Group reported that 65 million people were displaced from their homes mostly by war. Half of this figure is children. The top ten source countries of refugees as reported by the group are the Syrian Arab Republic, Afghanistan, South Sudan, Somalia, Sudan, Democratic Republic of Congo, Central African Republic, Myanmar, Eritrea and Colombia (The International Crisis Group 2016). While the causes of the displacement are a complex mix of socio, political and economic factors, fact remains that the failure to respond to the refugee crisis risks further conflict, triggering further refugee flows.

As right-wing politics takes ascendance in various parts of the world, what is now being witnessed is a backlash not just against refugees but also against migrants who very well may be documented and regular contributors to the economies of the states that they reside in. As per a report in *the Economic Times* dated on 16 December 2016, India is the top country of origin of international migrants in the world, and this report is based on data released by Pew Research (*Economic Times* 2016). The queer part about migration in the context of India is that it is a two- way flow. While India sends the maximum number of international migrants as outflows, India also receives a considerable number of international migrants as inflows. Most of the inflows to India are from neighbouring South Asian countries. In the absence of up to date and credible data, it becomes difficult to assess the exact scale of such inflows. However, if one takes the case of Nepal, which is one of the smaller and lesser developed countries in the South Asian region, as stated by the 1991 Census of Nepal, the migrant population of Nepal residing and/or working in India constituted 89.2 percent of the total migrants (Bhattrai 2007).

While the economic benefits of migration are known more widely, the behavioral-psychological benefits to the place of residence of migrants need to be studied in greater detail. What also makes an interesting case is the way migrants navigate across borders, challenging traditional notions of sovereignty and borders. In the north eastern region of India, where languages and ethnicities exist in abundance, such a case study of migration to the region becomes imperative.

Nepal and Northeast India in History

The history of the globe is one of migration, and the North-eastern region of India is no exclusion. Northeast India is one of the most heterogeneous linguistic and cultural regions of the world and has been a stage for a plurality of a transitional continuum from community and collectivity to nationality. Northeast India is the home of many nationalities, sub-nationalities, minority nationalities and ethnopolitical collectiveness that have been continuously moving through various formative and development phases. The region has around 430 languages and dialects of different language families that are used in a complex and wide-ranging ethnic and sociolinguistic configuration (Samuel 1993: 91).

Assam, the largest geographical state in the region possesses special significance for various reasons. Both culturally and politically, Assam is one of India's frontiers. Nevertheless, the Empires of the past had no more than a nodding acquaintance with Assam. In exploring relations between Nepal and Assam, it is observed that the history of the advent of the Nepalese in Assam is very different from that in places like Darjeeling, Sikkim and Uttaranchal. Assam in the chronicles of history is known as Kamrup. In the Puranic Age, Nepal and Kamrup comprised a single domain. Matsyendranath, a mystic yogi of Kamrup is commonly believed to have gone to Nepal and settled there. As stated by Devi (2007), the presence of the Nepalese in Assam is historical and their role in unification and economic development of this region is very crucial. (Devi 2007: 3005)

The Kamrup Kingdom had its boundaries right up to eastern Nepal in late 1520, and the two Kamrup Kings- Nidhwaj and Narayan had married Princesses of Nepal. As such, several sociological and historical studies reveal that there had been marital relationships between the peoples of Nepal and Assam from the period of Harsha Varmadeva (730- 750 A.D.) (Subba 2009: 216). The earliest references to the area which now is known as Assam are in the Mahabharata and the Puranas and in Tantric Literature, wherein it is referred to As Pragyajyotisha and Kamrupa. Pragyajyotisha, the term means the "land of eastern astrology," The early rulers of Assam name the capital as Pragyajyotishpur. Pusya Barman, who had assumed the title of Maharajadhiraja, was a contemporary of the Gupta monarch, Samudra Gupta (335-75 AD), whose Allahabad inscription records that Kamrup was on the eastern frontier of the Gupta Kingdom, and that its rulers accepted the suzerainty of the Guptas (Deka 2008: 103). Only after the decline of the Guptas, did Kamrup emerge as a powerful kingdom. Mahendra Barman, the fifth ruler of the Kamrup dynasty extended boundaries of the Kingdom considerably. During the reign of Kumar Bhaskar Barman, Hieun Tsang had visited Kamrup, and Hieun Tsang's description of the Kamrup forms an important source of study of the period.

From Buddhist records of the period, along with Greek accounts of the 11th century, the southern boundary of Pragyajyotisha was the Lohit Sagar, the western boundary was the Kousika River, the northern boundaries were the Bhutan hills and parts of Nepal. From the accounts of Hieun Tsang, it has been surmised that the Kingdom of Kamrup included a portion of Bihar, portions of Northern and Eastern Bengal and nearly the whole of Assam Valley. Some portions of Bengal were under Kamrupa from the time of Bhaskara Varman who ruled in the first half of the 6th century A.D. to the time of Harshadeva (725-750 A.D.) (Paul 1939: 33). Geographically, this region was a buffer zone between two different cultures during pre-Christian and early Christian era, i.e. of Indo-European and Euro- Chinese. The zone was more of a cultural bridge between South and South East Asia. As stated in the initial part of this work, the region was inhabited by the Kirats, who belonged to a Mongoloid stock. The region formed a trade route between India and China in about second century B.C.

The ancient link between Nepal and Assam was resurrected in modern times in the 19th century. Since the regime of Lord Bentinck as the Governor General of British India, several agreements, pacts, treaties, land accession were common factors that led the Nepalese to move towards the region of Northeast India, those of Kokrajhar, Bodoland Territorial Autonomous District (BTAD) or other areas of Goalpara (Subedy 2014: 122)

Trends of Nepali Migration and the Build up to the 21st Century

The British had selected many regions within Assam for the extraction of oil, coal, lime, tea plantation, road construction etc. Depopulation was a serious concern for the British under such circumstances. Therefore, the British recruited a large number of Nepalese from outside the state as workers. For assisting in various works of the company and the state, they were freely engaged as bearers, drivers, peons, porters etc. After retirement or while in service, they settled permanently in the vicinity of those industries or elsewhere in Assam (*Ibid.).*

Another significant reason behind the advent of the Nepalese in Assam lies in history again. Between 1817 and 1819, Assam was invaded twice by the Burmese. As a result of frequent Burmese invasions and attacks, socioeconomic conditions of the people of Assam became miserable to the extent that the then King Purandar Singh fled from Assam and sought help from the British East India Company to fight the Burmese. The British East India Company brought the Assam Light Infantry from Cuttack which comprised primarily of Gurkha soldiers. During the war on 5 March 1824, the Burmese soldiers were pushed back to within their own boundaries by the Gurkha soldiers. Soon enough, the Treaty of Yandaboo was signed in 1826 and Assam was brought under British administration and rule. The British East India Company insisted that the Gurkha soldiers reside in Assam even after retirement so that the forthcoming generations could also be recruited in the army.

Starting in the mid 19th century, Nepalese from the central hill areas have been continuously emigrating - most of them permanently. The central region of Nepal contains 60 percent of the country's total population, but only a quarter of the cultivated land of the country. Despite continuous emigration, Nepal's population doubled, which led to an acute economic and ecological crisis in the hill regions of Nepal. Even in the year 1900, over 250,000 Nepalese were living already in North India. This meant one out of every 20 Nepalese was living in North India. Most of these migrants were found to be working in factories or as watchmen or as domestic helps (Seddon, Gurung and Adhikari 1998). In the year 1901, the number of Nepalese immigrants in Assam stood at 21,347 which increased to 47,654 in 1911 and further to 70, 344 in 1921 and to 88, 306 in 1931. After independence, the number increased further, and in 1961, the number of Nepali migrants in Assam stood at 215213 (Chetry 2016: 23). As stated by Lopitha Nath, "Nepali colonial settlers in Northeast India are distinguished by a high level of integration with the local indigenous communities amongst whom they have lived for centuries" (Nath 2005: 58).

Despite the initial welcome and facilities offered by the British for Nepalese immigration in 1920, the British administration suddenly carried out an eviction operation in the now well known Kaziranga sanctuary and perpetrated several atrocities on the Nepalese immigrants settled there. It was not just the Nepali community which raised its head in revolt, but also the Assamese middle class. The same solidarity was witnessed in the course of India's freedom movement, beginning from the days of the non-cooperation movement. In India alone, by the year 1970, there were 1.5 million Nepalese, out of a population of 11.55 million in Nepal. The annual rate of migration in 1961 was 82,000 a year and 20,000 of these 82,000 remained in India permanently every year (Dutt 1981: 1053). The total number of Nepalese living outside Nepal is easily about 2.1 million, and the majority of these emigrants has settled in North India, and now comprises a working class whose presence is an accepted part of the landscape.

As such the history of Nepalese migration into India on the whole and into Northeast India is not new. The Diaspora again has undergone various waves of assimilations in the past and continues to undergo similar waves in the present. This paper seeks to trace the history and the current challenges the Nepali speaking populace in Assam faces- more particularly in Karbi Anglong, which vies to be a state based solely on the Karbi identity.

The introductory section of this work has outlined the ancient ties between Assam and Nepal. The following section looks into the issues faced by people of Nepali origin living in Assam.

Nature of border between India and Nepal

Migration from Nepal in the contemporary era, as stated earlier, dates to the 19th century when several Nepalese migrated and joined various ranks of the British army; besides having been utilised by the colonial British government to address issues of depopulation in Northeast India through a repopulation of the area with Nepali populace. In international relations, states are based on territory, and the respect for the territorial integrity of states within recognised borders is an important principle of international relations. Several of the borders in the 21st century are outcomes of wars in the past or effects of colonialism. The case of the border between India and Nepal is an interesting one, because it is an open border. Nepal shares approximately 1700 kilometers of open borders with India in the East, South and West. A bilateral friendship treaty was signed between the two countries in 1950, and it was agreed that the citizens of the two countries can travel and work freely across the border and have to be treated the same way as native citizens are. Currently, approximately one million Nepalese work in India, and most of them are unskilled labourers (Bhattrai 2007). According to the 2001 Census of Nepal, 762,181 persons were abroad, with a significant percentage in India. Several small-scale studies conducted in specific regions, districts, villages or cities suggest that mobility across the Indo- Nepal border is extremely high. In a survey conducted in 1997 in five border towns of Nepal, seven out of ten adult men stated that they visited India almost every month (Tamang, Puri, Nepal, Shrestha 2006: 51). A 1999 assessment conducted in 20 percent of the villages of Doti—a far-western hill district where migration was common— it was found that at least one member of the family from half of the households had worked abroad, nearly all (94 percent) in India (Poudel, Okumura, Sharma, Tandukar and Wakai 2004: 32).

In the last ten years, the Government of Nepal declared that migration of Nepalese people for labour and employment abroad had become the backbone of the country's economy and the highest source of revenues. The migration of citizens out of the country is more than two and a half centuries old, and it began with the recruitment of Gurkha soldiers in the 19th century by the British East India Company in the British Indian Army. As stated by Nath, these Gurkha soldiers originally belonged to ethnic Nepali communities of the Gurung, Magar from Western Nepal and Tamang from Eastern Nepal. They derived their name from the Gurkha ruler who had established a unified Nepali state in 1768 (Nath 2010: 18). The colonial government recognised the versatility of the soldiers and sent them as far as China, Crimea, Greece and South Africa.

In Northeast India, the Gurkha soldiers were a part of the Sylhet Operations as part of the Cuttack Legion. This, later on, came to be known as the Assam Light Infantry. Within a period of six years (1833- 1839), almost one-third of the battalions in the Assam Light Infantry came to be composed of Gurkhas. The Cachar Levy which was the predecessor of the Assam Rifles liberally enlisted the Gurkhas, and their number in the army was almost half of the total number of soldiers. The emblem of the Assam Rifles, in fact, is the Nepali *Khukuri.*[1]

In the First World War, around 243,000 men from Nepal enlisted in the British Army, and an additional 160,000 were recruited during the Second World War (Gurung and Adhikari 2010: 101). In 2003, there were about 48,000 Nepalese is serving in the Indian army and about 150,000 pensioners (*Ibid.*).

After India's independence, a lot of labour migration followed the previously treaded terrains of the Gurkha soldiers, and the Nepalese headed for the areas on the North and North eastern border areas, where the colonial British government had allowed Gurkha settlements. The Kumaon and Garhwal hills, Darjeeling in North Bengal, Sikkim, Northeast India and the hilly areas of Uttar Pradesh became the key destinations for the Nepali labourers. They found employment in Assam and in Darjeeling and also worked in an array of jobs in the erstwhile British Hill stations in Northern India.

The migration of labour from Nepal soon spread to more newly emerging townships and cities where labour was in demand. This flow of labour across borders was facilitated by the Indo Nepal Friendship Treaty of 1950 and by the ample scope for employment created by the modernising economy of independent India.

The 1952/54, 1981, 1991 and 2001 census data of Nepal show that Nepali citizens have regularly emigrated to India. Migration to India accounted for 79.4 percent of all emigrants from Nepal in 1952/54, an overpowering 93.11 percent in 1981, 89.21 percent in 1991 and 77.28 percent in 2001. The number of migrants to India has nearly quadrupled in just five decades; figures from the Central Bureau of Statistics cite 157,323 in 1952/54 to 589,050 in 2001

(Sharma 2010). According to Kaustavmoni Boruah, another important reason for the migration for out-migration from Nepal to Northeast India, and to Assam, in particular, is that the neo-Assamese middle class and the representative government contributed a great deal to the influx of people from outside the region- which included people from Nepal. The Assamese middle class, with a view of employing cheap labour in their fields and homesteads. The conservative section of the Assamese Hindu middle class encouraged Nepali people, in particular, to immigrate to Assam, and in this way, the Nepali people got access to the forest lands and the char areas of the Brahmaputra Valley (Boruah 1980: 46). Boruah adds that often Assamese Hindus recruited a large number of Nepalese for agriculture and household work, who after a certain period settled down permanently in Assam.

In exploring the issue of identity, the case of Nepalese in Karbi Anglong becomes interesting. Karbi Anglong has been vying to be a separate state for a considerable period of time. However, the non Karbi populace of Karbi Anglong is also significant in numbers and the question of these groups' identities in a place which wants to base itself only on the Karbi identity and become a totally Karbi state becomes interesting to explore. The following section discusses the question of Nepalese in Karbi Anglong.

The 'Nepali' identity in Karbi Anglong

The largest state in India's northeast is Assam, which is divided into 23 districts in all. Karbi Anglong is the largest of these and is one of the two autonomous districts under the Indian Constitution. The other such autonomous district in Assam is that of the neighbouring North Cachar Hills. Karbi Anglong was accorded the autonomous status since it is inhabited by various indigenous groups, who are classified under the ambit of Scheduled Tribes under the Indian Constitution. These 'indigenous' groups were outside the purview of direct administration of taxation and direct taxation in the period of British colonial rule. After India's independence in 1947, after several political and constitutional deliberations, several areas were demarcated as autonomous areas. The rationale behind the move was the need to allow indigenous communities the freedom to retain their traditions and customary laws, without becoming victims of rapid developmental changes. Thus, currently, Karbi Anglong is governed by a council and contests over resources and territory continue to rage. According to information provided by the Council, the *Karbis* are the most dominant indigenous group in the district. Other indigenous groups like *Bodos, Kukis, Dimasas, Khasis, Man- Tai, Tiwa, Nagas* and *Garos* also are residents of the district.

Besides the indigenous groups, Karbi Anglong also has a large number of Assamese people and comparatively new settlers from Nepal and from the Gangetic plains of India. In 1952, the Constituent Assembly bestowed the Sixth Schedule status upon the tribal hill districts of Assam, which is why Karbi Anglong was in turn endowed with the district and regional councils. Karbi Anglong, has three subdivisions, Diphu, Hamren and Bokajan. The four police *thanas* in Karbi Anglong are Diphu, Baithalangso, Howraghat and Bokajan. The autonomous council is provided with some executive, legislative and judicial powers, and there is an Executive Committee of the Council with executive members, principal secretary and secretaries and chief executive member, which is a replica of a state legislative assembly, although with limited powers. The executive members are elected, with at least four being nominated by the governor, while the secretaries are civil servants appointed by the Government of Assam. The district sends one member to the national parliament in New Delhi.

Due to its location in southern Assam, Karbi Anglong has a porous undefined border with Meghalaya and with the west and with Assam in general. The Karbis are the dominant tribe in the district. However, Karbi Anglong has other blocks and villages which are manned by people of other tribes and ethnicities. The 25 Mile Nepali Basti in Diphu circle of Karbi Anglong, for example, is a small village located with a total of 20 families residing.

Migration in Karbi Anglong

Migration has been an important aspect of life in Karbi Anglong. After India attained independence and the demarcation of the autonomous district of Karbi Anglong in particular in 1952, there was a steady inflow of cultivators from neighbouring districts and states. The largest number of people who migrated to the region was primarily Hindi speaking people from the Gangetic plains. Inflows from districts like Nagaon and Golaghat was also witnessed. Till 1947, migration into Karbi Anglong was relatively low. In 1961, when Karbi Anglong was a part of the United Mikir and North Cachar Hills district, the migrant population was around one hundred thousand; out of which most were rural migrants, since the only two urban centres in the twin districts were Diphu and

Haflong. Diphu now is the headquarter of Karbi Anglong, while Haflong is the district headquarter of North Cachar Hills.

Despite all the ethnic turmoil and the lack of rapid development in the region, migration has been a persistent feature of existence in Karbi Anglong. What is interesting to note is that in terms of linguistic identities, the Nepali settlers have generally retained their language- yet have adopted Assamese firmly as their first language. As stated in the earlier part of this paper, the Nepali settlers in India are distinguished by a high level of integration with the local indigenous communities in India, amongst whom they have lived for centuries. This holds true even in Karbi Anglong. In terms of socio -economic profile, it is noted that the average Nepali is not part of the white collar labour force. One of the most pertinent reasons for this is that Karbi Anglong, in general, is not a rapidly growing economic entity. Other reasons include the lack of education or the lack of the will for higher education.

Given the renewal of demands for Karbi Anglong being upgraded to a separate state, members of various communities in the district are experiencing heightened fear, and in 2013, a delegation of the Karbi Anglong Bengali Jatiya Manch met chief minister Tarun Gogoi to ensure that isolation of the Bengali community does not take place in the vent of Karbi Anglong actually becoming a separate state. During interviews with Nepali speaking people in the region, a similarity in terms of uncertainty about the future coupled with fear was encountered. Unlike the Bengali community of the district, the Nepali speaking people have not yet organised themselves into a group that could voice their fears and apprehensions regarding the formation of a separate Karbi state. However, the fact remains that the same amount of uncertainty and apprehension regarding Karbi Anglong as a separate state remains among members of the Nepali speaking community as well.

Conclusion

Structuralism posits that elements of human culture have to be understood in terms of their relationship to a larger, overarching system or structure. This helps to uncover structures that underlie all human activities, perceptions and feelings. Alternatively, as posited by Simon Blackburn, the phenomena of human lives are not intelligible except through their interrelations. These relations constitute a structure, and behind local variations in the surface phenomena, there are constant laws of abstract culture.

In analysing the case of the Nepali speaking population in Karbi Anglong, the overarching system or structure is that of Karbi Anglong as "home". The relationship between the Nepali resident and the structure comprises of language, mixes of languages, and the identity as a resident of Karbi Anglong. This relationship, in turn, is comprised of constant laws of abstract nature.

What happens in the case of state formation on the lines of ethnic identity is the loss of identity and residence of 'others'. While states formed on ethnic lines aims at inclusion, what happens in the process is the exclusion of those who are considered as 'others'. Additionally what happens in the case of newly formed states, as has been witnessed in cases of Jharkhand and Chattisgarh is that levels of development and the allocation of administrative relations with the Centre continue to be problematic for a considerable time period, which in turn defeats the purpose of the formation of a separate state to increase rates of development.

Be it Nepali settlers or Bengali settlers in Karbi Anglong, the fact remains that most of these erstwhile migrated communities are now in their third or fourth generations of existence, and have completely assimilated to the place. An exclusion of these groups in the case of the formation of a Karbi state based only on the Karbi identity will be further detrimental to the already low growth rates and development of the district.

References

Bhattrai, Raju (2007), "International migration, multi-local livelihoods and human security: Perspectives from Europe, Asia and Africa", Institute of Scoail Studies, The Netherlands.

Boruah, Kaustavmoni, "Foreigners" in Assam and Assamese Middle Class", *Social Scientist*, 8 No.11 (1982): 45-47.

Chetry, Sanjib Kumar (2016) "Nepal is in Assam: A Historical Perspective (1816- 1985)", *Research Journal of Language, Literature and Humanities*, 22-25.

Deka, Basant. *Assam: Land and People*. Guwahati: K C Das College, 2008.

Devi, Monimala. "Economic History of Nepali Migration and Settlement in Assam", *Economic and Political Weekly*, 42 No.29 (2007).

Dutt, Srikanth. "Migration and Development: The Nepalese in the Northeast." *Economic and Political Weekly* 6 No. 24 (1981): 1053-1055.

Economic Times (2016), "India Top Country of Origin of International Migrants", 16 December 2016, Washington, URL: http://economictimes.indiatimes.com/nri/

visa-and-immigration/india-top-country-of-origin-of-international-migrants-pew/articleshow/56014770.cms Accessed on May 15, 2017

Gurung, Ganesh and Adhikari, Jaganath The Prospects and Problems of Foreign Labour Migration in Migrant Workers and Human Rights Out-Migration from South Asia In Migrant *Workers and Human Rights,* edited by Pong-Sul Ahn 100-128. Geneva: International Labour Organisation, 2010.

International Crisis Group (2016) "What's Driving the Global Refugee Crisis?", URL: https://www.crisisgroup.org/global/global-refugee-crisis-statement-board-trustees-international-crisis-group Accessed on May 15, 2017

Kansakar, Vidya Bir Singh. "Nepal- India Open Border: Prospects, Problems and Challenges". *Nepal Democracy*. 4 September, 2014. http://nepaldemocracy.org/

Nath, Lopita. "Migrants in Flight: Conflict Induced Internal Displacement of Nepal is in Northeast India", *Peace and Democracy in South Asia,* 1 No.1 (2005): 56- 72.

Nath, Lopita. "The Strength of Weak Ties: Role of Networks in Nepali Migration to South and Southeast Asia 1900- 2000", *Bodhi,* 4 No.1 (2010): 18-47

Paul, P. L. *Early History of Bengal,* Calcutta: Vanga and Vangala, 1939.

Poudel, Jimba; Okumura, J; Sharma M; Poudel, Tandukar K; and Wakai (2004) "Migration in far western Nepal: a time bomb for a future HIV/AIDS epidemic", *Tropical Doctor,* 34(30): 1-30.

Samuel, John (1993) "Language and Nationality in North-East India." Economic and Political Weekly, 28 No.3/4 (1993).

Subedy, Shyam. "Advent of the Nepali People to the Present Day B.T.C. Assam", *Pratidhwani the Echo,* II N0. IV (2014): 121-124

Seddon, David; Gurung, Ganesh and Adhikari, Jagannath (1998) "Fireign Labour Migration and Remittance Economy of Nepal", Himalaya: The Journal FOR Nepal and Himalayan Studies, Vol. 18: No. 2, Article 7

Sharma, Sanjay. "Lost in Enumeration." *Kathmandu Post,* August 4, 2010. Accessed 12 November, 2014, URL: http://www.ekantipur.com/the-kathmandu-post/2011/08/04/oped/lost-in-enumeration/224817.html

Samuel, John "Language and Nationality in North-East India." *Economic and Political Weekly,* 28 No.3/4 (1993): 91-92.

Subba, Tanka B. "Living the Nepali Diaspora in India: An Autobiographical Essay", *Zeitschrift für Ethnologie,* 133, No.2 (2009): 213-232.

Tamang, A; Puri, M.; Nepal, B; Shrestha, D. "Sexual risk behavior and risk perception of STDs/AIDS transmission among men in five border towns of Nepal", (2006) Centre for Research on Environment Health and Population Activities.

Endnotes

1. The *Khukuri* (खुकुरी in Nepali) is a Nepalese knife which has an inwardly curved edge, similar to the machete. It is used as a toll and as a weapon in Nepal and in neighbouring countries of South Asia. It is a characteristic weapon of the Nepalese Army, the Royal Gurkha Rifles and of all Gurkha regiments. English speakers refer commonly to the weapon as a "Gurkha blade" or a "Gurkha knife".

Chapter Three

International Labour Migration, Remittance and Impacts on Livelihood: A Case Study of Dalit Community in Western Nepal

Prakash Upadhyay

Abstract

A product of various social, cultural and historical processes, the caste dimension of Nepali society intertwined with development and livelihood is an issue of great anthropological interest. Excluded from national development mainstream due to caste discriminations, bigotry and extreme Hinduism, the so-called low caste Dalits are considered untouchables in orthodox Hindu socio-cultural model and has been historically victimized by state and marginalized in a predominant caste ridden and priest ridden orthodox Nepali society. Consequently, they are vulnerable to poverty and backwardness. Most Dalit groups have their traditional occupational skills but nowadays, owing to limited markets access and availability of cheap international products their traditional occupations has been threatened that has worsened their livelihood options. The lower educational status and caste discrimination has also hindered to obtain better jobs in Nepal consequently compelling them to international migration for labour. Despite remittance's role in lessening caste discriminations and supporting families' livelihood, there has been a modest improvement in Dalit households' human, educational and financial assets. The present scenario of meager educational, economic and human status, trivial involvement in social and development sectors are the proofs of inability of remittances to address Dalits genuine livelihood problems. In the absence of productive and sustainable remittance use, foreign dependency has increased which is creating insecurities in Dalit livelihood. International labour migration has become an addictive behaviour. Formulation and effective implementation of pro-poor employment strategies, giving continuity to traditional but refined skill-based occupations at home and investment oriented productive remittance use policies are prerequisite.

Introduction

The population census of Nepal 2011 records 26.5 million population (81.3 percent Hindus) comprising 48.5 percent male and 51.5 percent female. There are 125 different caste/ethnic groups speaking 123 languages exhibiting immense cultural and religious diversities. These groups include people of Indo-Aryan origin, having traditional caste groups according to the Hindu caste system, and the ethnic groups, mostly of Tibeto-Mongoloid origin (CBS 2011). *Dalits* or low caste untouchables are Hindu groups of Indo-Aryan origin from both hill and terai comprising 14.1 percent of Nepal's total population according to CBS 2011 population statistics despite Dalit civil society claims of 20 percent. There are different subsets within the Dalit community. The Dalit Commission (2002) noted 28 cultural groups of Dalits from different sub-caste groups from the hills (*Hill Dalits*), the Tarai (*Tarai/Madhesi Dalits*) and indigenous Dalit Newar community of Kathmandu. There are four major groups of Dalits in hills-*Kami/ Sunar* (Ironsmith/Goldsmith), *Damai* (Tailor), *Sarki* (Cobbler) and *Gaine* (Musician). They are the artisan/occupational caste groups possessing unique traditional skills.

Dalits are the most marginalized, backward and poorest of poor in Nepal. Historically victimized by the state and considered untouchables in orthodox Hindu social-cultural model, Dalits are susceptible to poverty and backwardness (NHDR 2014). They are disadvantaged community forced to holdup at the bottom of the social structure and excluded from national development mainstream due to caste discrimination and extreme Hinduism. Historically, the caste system was introduced in Nepal by the Aryans of Gangetic plains of India who imposed a stratified Hindu caste system in Nepal during medieval ages by superior military power, ideological warfare, and by hard-nosed shrewd diplomacy. They enforced strict caste regulations in the rest of Nepal except in Kathmandu valley which was having its own caste system introduced by King Jayasthiti Malla in 14th century.

The caste system has resulted in the caste-based splitting up of Nepalese society and the marginalization of Dalits in political, economic, social, cultural and educational spheres of the mainstream. Though equipped with traditional occupational skills like iron and gold smithy, tailoring, shoemaking etc, in the recent days, due to the ignorance of their arts and skills by the market, lack of modernization in traditional occupations, limited access to markets, availability of cheap international products, many Dalits are abandoning their traditional occupation. This has worsened their livelihoods the means of securing the basic necessities of life-food, water, shelter, clothing etc. The lower status of education and caste discrimination has also become barriers to obtain better jobs for Dalits, consequently preparing the ground for their migration abroad for labour. Numerous Dalits have gone abroad as labourers to countries like Qatar, Saudi Arab, Dubai, Bahrain, Malaysia and European countries etc. But, despite remittance earning, there has been very little improvement in their human, educational and financial assets despite remittance being a central pillar of their economy for supporting household economy.

South Asia's worst malaise, poverty, lack of infrastructure development, sudden rise in young population, greater connectivity with the outer worlds due to globalization and, most importantly, gap in wages have encouraged the 1.5 million plus people every year from the region to leave for destination countries for earning (*Rising Nepal* 2017). Historically, international labor migration formally began in Nepal in 1815 AD with the recruitment of Nepali youth in The British Brigade of Gurkha (Gurung 1983; Thieme, Susan & Wyss 2005). However, it was only after the promulgation of the Foreign Employment Act in 1989, that the Nepali workers started to migrate abroad for remittance earning. Kollmair et al. (2006) argues that this resulted in large streams of international migration outside of India. According to the Government of Nepal (2014) estimates there may be as many as three million Nepalese, or about 10 percent of the total population, working abroad and earning remittance. The percentage of migrants is much higher for young people and for men.

Remittance is the money or foreign currency obtained from abroad after paying physical or mental labour. With the increased volume of international migration, the volume of remittances has been increasing in the last many years in Nepal despite *the Himalayan Times* Newspaper report (2016) portrayal of unsatisfactory picture of remittance flow. According to this latest report remittance inflows to Nepal rose by just 5.7 percent to Rs. 342.2 billion in the first half of 2016/17, compared to its growth of 17.3 percent in the same period of the previous year. But, the reduction in poverty owing to remittance has helped in diversification in livelihoods, greater ownership and acquirement of assets and capitals. Lokshin et.al (2007 2010) found that increased migration for foreign work contributed about one-fifth of poverty reduction in Nepal during 1995-2004 but it had positive and insignificant effects on inequality.

According to World Bank (2016), excluding the remittances received through informal channels, the remittances received through the formal channels accounted for about 29 percent of Nepalese GDP. Nepal stands as the third largest remittance recipient in its contribution to GDP in the world. At the present remittances has become an important source of household income for Nepalese (Adhikari 2001; Hoermann & Kollmair 2009). Higher growth of labour force and limited employment opportunities outside the farm sector is the major factor contributing to large scale out migration from Nepal. The escalating labour force unmatched by additional job creation, low salary and high demand of labour in the industrializing Asian and Gulf countries are the other contributing factors. Additionally, poverty and food scarcity are strong push factors for increasing outmigration in the context of Dalits.

The utilization of remittances in Nepal for the improvement of the living standard has been documented by several studies (Wahidin 1989, Seddon et al, 2001 and Department of Women Development 2003). Remittance are typically spent on land and housing. These are safe investment for the households, but in macroeconomic terms, they are non-productive assets, with no lasting impact on the country's actual income. Thus, while the remittances are beneficial at household and community level, they cannot help long term development of the country without its planned management. The saving rate amongst the Nepalese workers is lower as the majority of them are employed in low paying jobs and their marginal propensity to consume is relatively higher. Only the small proportion of the migrants uses the remittance directly for productive investment like agriculture, manufacturing and trade. The major forms of remittance investments are on children's education, reinvestment for further migration and for lending money (Lokshin et.al 2010). The resources and expertise of the returned migrants could also be a good resource for country's economic development. Nepal does not have authentic data on the numerical dimension of the returned migrants.

In Nepal Rastra Bank Survey conducted in 2007 on 832 households in 8 districts (half of them from Far Western Development Region) of Nepal, the majority of the families were dependent on remittance money. Regarding the use of remittance and skills of returned migrants, the major portion of the remittance was used for meeting household use and to pay back loans borrowed earlier to go abroad. Remittance money was also spent on land and housing. These are safe investment but in microeconomic terms they are non-industrious assets. Likewise, 47 percent of the returned migrants had learned new skill while working abroad, but only 16 percent had used the skill for income generating activities after their return. The survey concluded that the remittances was not beneficial at household and community level and were unable to help long term development of the country without its strategic management.

The remittances-and-development literature locates remittances as a prospective, however, problematic source of economic development. Deliberations in this field twirl around two themes (Taylor et.al 1996): (1) how remittances are invested in migrants' places of origin; and (2) whether remittances reduce or exacerbate inequality. Researchers have sought to better understand who promotes, pursues, and benefits from remittances. Raising question why one group benefits more from remittances than another could unlock a more political discussion of the relationship between remittances and development, however studies seldom move in that direction. Taylor et.al (1996) argues that one of the primary weaknesses of the remittances and development studies is that they focus nearly exclusively on economic impacts of remittances while questions of politics, society, religion, and culture are relegated to the margins. The remittances-and-development studies commonly blames migrants for failing to make rational, productive decisions about their remittances as remittances are spent primarily on consumption – on fulfilling daily needs –while only a small portion is invested in productive sector. Some articulate distress that remittances lose their power as a tool of development if they are wasted on mere consumption. However, obviously normative claims like these glimmers sharp responses. Migrants may not be the most appropriate agents for contending with underdevelopment. Indeed, individuals often seek out migration as a survival strategy since their places of origin lack meaningful development in the first place (Taylor 1999). As the Dalits of Nepal were socially, culturally and economically victimized by the state historically, hence,in order to envisage the impacts of remittances on development and livelihood, it may be necessary to assess their social, cultural, historical and personal conditions as well as economic constraints. Dalit migrants' intentions regarding the purposes and uses of their remittances may have an interior reason that is reliable and reasoned, despite deviating from capitalist prospects of rational investment in productive sector. Previous studies on remittances-and-development leave behind modest space for considering this possibility. Hence, this current study on Dalit community endeavors to look into this by referring to logics based on primary data derived from the field.

Objective and Methods

This study is pedestaled on the use pattern and effects of remittance on the livelihood of Dalit people. It tries to dig out the veracity of their livelihood and comprehend the assorted condition of Dalit livelihood influenced by the remittance. The main objective is to examine the trend of international labour migration in the Dalit community and the impacts of remittance on their livelihood.

Based on primary field data from a small sample of Dalit households collected from a part of western Nepal, this study was conducted in Salyan Village Development Committee (VDC) of Kaski district in the western hills of Nepal. This is the largest Dalit settlement in this region with 135 Dalit households. These 135 Dalit households was the universe of the study, of which 86 Dalit households solely dependent on remittance, were selected for the study. At the first stage of sampling, households listing was done to identify the eligible respondents (informants). After households listing only 86 respondents (one each from 86 households) were chosen for interview. The respondents were the household heads (81 females and 5 males) from each remittance receiving household. These household heads are the key decision makers in their family. Data was collected by semi-structured individual interviews (closed and open-ended questions) and observation. Closed ended questions were used for the collection of household and individual information, while open ended questions were used to understand the remittance use pattern and its effects on livelihood. The field work for data collection was accomplished during 8-26 March 2017.

Theoretical Discourses on the Interplay between Migration, Remittance and Livelihood

Pedestaled on the theoretical perspectives of New Economics of Labor Migration (NELM) framework, this study examines the remittance receipt by migrant Dalit households. The neoclassical microeconomics focuses on individuals' relative earning potentials in origin and destination with a belief that individuals migrate when the expected gain from migrating to a destination is greater than that from staying in the origin (Hay 1980). But according to NELM, migration of individuals is a family-based decision and is an attempt to diversify household income portfolios to protect against risk and gain access to capital in order to finance consumer and productive purchases (Stark, 1991; Stark & Bloom 1985; Stark & Taylor 1991). Accordingly, the choice to migrate by household members is a family approach to reduce risks/uncertainties. By making such choice and decision, a household makes an investment on migration and in return the household expects to receive remittances (Sana & Massey 2005).

On sending remittances, there are three arguments to explain whether a migrant will remit or not: altruism, self-interest, and insurance and risk sharing (Agarwal & Horowitz 2002; Arun & Ulku 2011). It is assumed that migrants are fretful about their family members back home. Zai Liang & Ma (2013) argue that migrants send remittances for the well-being of households' members who are left behind (altruism motive). It is also anticipated that a household will send members to destinations with high earning potentials with the hope of receiving higher remittances. However, Seddon et al. (1998) argues that the destinations with higher earning potentials are most likely hardest to be reached. But when the migrants are successful to get there and get a work, the earning prospective are higher. Migrant's earning is one of the important determinants of whether one remits or not and the amount of remittances sent (Arun & Ulku 2011). The earning potentials of migration differ by destinations hence it is expected that the remittances received by a household from migrants and its uses will also differ by migrants' destinations.

International Labour Migration, Remittance Uses and Impacts on Dalits Livelihood

Of the sampled 86 household heads in the study area, 82 (95.5 percent) households are of *Kami*, 3 (3.5 percent) households are of *Damai* and only 1 house (1.0 percent) of *Sarki* (Cobbler) family. Of these 84 household heads (97.5 percent) are married and 2 (2.5 percent) are unmarried. The average family size of household is 5 members each household. All the 81 female household heads (respondents) are housewives involved in household chores and agricultural works. As majority of productive males are working abroad only 5 males head their families (their wives are working abroad) of which 2 are involved in skilled occupation of iron smithy in the village whereas 3 males are jobless. Large portion of female respondents inactive from professional economic earning depicts the picture of high dependency on remittances. It also denotes that owing to the easy availability of foreign remittance they are reluctant to look for any occupation at home. They lack concrete information and knowledge on remittance use patterns in a proper way.

Among the 86 households, 42 (49.0 percent) have their members working in Qatar and 27 (31.3 percent) in Saudi Arab. Similarly, 15 (17.7 percent) are working in Malaysia, Dubai and Kuwait and the rest are in Spain and South Korea. The growing foreign migrants and accumulation of remittance has brought noteworthy changes in Dalit livelihood pattern in households and in the community. Labour migration has proved to be an effective strategy for livelihood adaptation for generating financial and human capital hence contributing to poverty alleviation. Most of the Dalit migrant labourers send remittance 30,000 to 45,000 Nepali rupees (300-450 US dollars) per month to their homes. International migration and remittance incomes have substantially contributed to the economic development of their families and have a significant and a positive impact on the everyday socio-economic life. The entire family is involved with sharing and trading off the costs and benefits of remitting. Remittance incomes have contributed to families' economic development, changed life-styles, improved living standards, developed confidence to reduce poverty and enabled challenging of caste-based discrimination to some extent. Work migration has been a part of a family adaptive strategy used to diversify the family's pattern of labour use, reduce the risk and dependence on a single economic activity and maximize family rather than individual welfare as claimed by Stark and Bloom (1985).

Despite the differences in receiving remittances, monthly familial expenses vary depending on family size and expenses behavior. Majority of households (70 percent) have the monthly expenses (to fulfill their basic needs) a little bit less than the monthly remittances received. The major spending of remittance is on food, children's education (in private English Boarding schools which are usually costly), household expenses viz. purchasing attires, medicines, house repairing, celebration of festivals or even procuring agricultural land. The concept of religion is more related with emotion and sentiments that drives Dalits towards lofty spending in festivals. Majority of Dalit families spend remittance money lavishly in various festivals as *Teej* (a festival of Hindu women), *Dashain* (Durga

Puja) and Deepawali. Dalit families spend up to Nepali rupees 25,000 in these festivals annually. This signifies that there is the practice of celebrating festivals with pomp and show and with ostentations. The utilization of the remittance is lacking in productive sectors that could have enhanced their socio-economic status. But the remittances have enabled the left-behind family members to live a prosperous life. The most direct way in which remittances is contributing to Dalit economic and social development is the improvement in the living standards of the families. Remittances has improved the living standard of the household enabling a higher level of consumption and increased educational opportunities for the children. Consumption by itself is not a productive activity however the increased consumption by households has improved their productivity by improving health or improved the capacity of young Dalit children in these households to learn and hence acquire a better education, which can contribute to societal development. The improvement in education opportunities for the rest of the family members is beneficial to the household.

Only thirty percent of Dalit households were able to make a good saving of the remittances received. They have taken the membership of saving groups or have bank accounts to deposit their money. Also, they are able to invest their money for various economic purposes to accumulate or increase their property. This economic strengthening has helped Dalits in building social relations with the so-called upper caste people through money lending and involvement in various rituals (birthday celebrations and marriages) that has resulted in the reduction of caste-based discriminations to some extent, and has assisted to support their bargaining capacity, mental, physical and social development.

Traditionally, victimized owing to caste bigotry, majority of Dalits were landless squatters previously or were the landless peasants working for so-called Hindu landlords. But foreign remittance has helped them in acquiring land. Many Dalits households have used the remittances for adding land. 54 (63.0 percent) households possess 1000-2000 sq m and 4 (4.6 percent) households have 2000-4000 sq m landholdings. 9 (10.4) households have 4000-6000 sq m and the rest 22 percent possess more than 6000-8000 sq m landholdings. From this data, we can see that there are sharp differences in landholding pattern in Dalit settlement. This situation is directing less landholding households towards insecure livelihood and supporting economic inequality within Dalit communities. Concurring to the theoretical perspective of NELM framework, the earning potentials of migration differ by destinations (e.g. the migrants working in South Korea, Spain, Malaysia send higher remittances), and hence the remittances received by a household determined the quantity of landholding at households level. Remittance uses has also helped many to construct houses. In the absence of remittances, it would have been problematic for Dalits to maintain their family expenses.

Although, there are economic, social and cultural reasons behind international migration as labourers, this has become an *addictive trend* in Dalit community. Rather than choosing any occupation in Nepal, Dalits prefer a foreign job which is a dangerous trend that is killing their traditional occupations and has accelerated foreign dependency. However, there has been a noteworthy impact on and contributions to the social security and economic development of Dalit families, more specifically remittances sent back to migrants' families has played an imperative role in alleviating paucity and improving livelihoods status, fulfilling basic needs, changing their living standards, improving their access to better education for their children and improved healthcare. Owing to economic empowerment, they are more confident than ever, and can take any decision owing to *social remittances* viz. the ideas, behaviours, identities, and social capital that has flown from remittance destination country communities. Similarly, owing to remittance they are at better position to add social capital i.e. win others trust and increase prestige, dignity, social response, and morality in the society. But, in the name of going abroad for foreign jobs many Dalits have been deceived by the agents -both legal and illegal agencies. It is essential that the government must mull over strict policies and implement these effectively so that Dalits can feel secure and confident if they intend to go abroad.

Human capital is the skill, knowledge and ability to work in a proper way. Financial capital, in terms of access to employment and earnings, is strongly dependent on adequate human capital. In turn, human capital is decidedly dependent on adequate nutrition, health care, safe environmental condition, and education. However, majority Dalits doesn't have much consciousness for good nutrition, education, health and skills. The awareness to get education is extremely low with 36 percent literacy rate of sampled Dalit household heads. Also, awareness on health and safe environmental condition is extremely low on the part of majority populace. There is the acute shortage of human resource (man) with only few young men left in the village. Also, they have insignificant involvement in social, development and economic sectors in their locality. Agricultural productivity has decreased because of reduced quantity of human labour. Due to the lack of labour force (active working male), the size of livestock holding is narrowing down in the village. Most of the Dalit households have abandoned agriculture and reduced the size of the livestock after their family member's migration abroad for labour. Hence, labour migration has created negative effect on agriculture and animal husbandry.

Sociologists believe that the stage of acute poverty, backwardness and suppression for a long time produce *culture of poverty*-- that is a culture shared by the downtrodden and the backwards. The term culture of poverty was first used by Oscar Lewis in 1968 while conducting study in Central America. The culture of poverty, thus, is a design or a *style for living*, which is transmitted from one generation to next and which influences all aspects of individual's life. Maltreated by the state and suppressed by caste based discriminations for centuries, the Dalit families are the victims of *culture of poverty* that have negative effects on their communities. Hence, Dalit households are facing meticulous challenges in benefiting from remittances that are linked to the specific situation of their lives. For example, they have very poor educational status, high expenses and have very meager involvement in social, development and economic sectors despite remittances uses. Emergence of remittance dependent *bountiful* culture has become a part of their life. School dropout is quite high among the Dalit students. Early marriage is also a big problem. Alcohol use is rampant. Among the 86 households, 56 (65 percent) households have already experienced bitter experiences of alcohol use. Not only males' even females have the regular habit of alcohol and excessive tobacco use. Smoking is a major problem responsible for various types of health hazards. Alcohol use has resulted in kidney and heart ailments in many Dalit male and female. Alcoholism is also one form of social hazards which shows that they don't have sufficient knowledge about good health. In such households, there will be more economic crisis and poor social development and that may lead to indecent utilization of earned remittance. Also, there will be a compulsion for medical treatment and will have to invest remittance money on medical treatment. Family quarrel owing to alcohol use and the poor emotional attachment between the migrants and their family members is a foremost problem. 12 (14.0 percent) households have the problem of family quarrels owing to alcohol uses and poor emotional attachment between the migrant and family members especially between spouses. But, 72 (83.7 percent) households have no any problem of family quarrel and have a healthy family life.

In broad-spectrum remittances beyond certain negative ramifications, have positive effects on the wellbeing of recipient families- fulfilling basic needs and has helped combat poverty that was virtually impossible for the Dalits previously. Remittance income has assisted Dalits in getting relief from their financial worries and making a better living in the society where they were deprived economically, culturally and socially for centuries. Beyond contributing to social change, remittance has contributed to economic development, improved living standards, changed life-styles and boosted confidence level. The Dalit migrants' family members staying behind at home are enjoying a privileged standard of living through the remittances. Labour migration has also become a part of the family adaptive strategy to diversify the family's pattern of labour use to maximize family welfare. The lost labour at home was compensated by remittances from migrants. Also, the remittance has provided impetus for human development in different ways. In addition to economic remittances, it has added to new ideas, behaviours, identities, and social prestige owing to economic empowerment. The consumption pattern of the remittance-receiving households could be characterized as an investment in human capital, but at the same time it may lead to dependency on foreign employment if the productive use is not realized. Remittance has helped condense poverty and increased the access to health and education services but remittance has not been utilized for productive investment and entrepreneurship which in turn could have increased job opportunities in the local community that would have contributed to long term sustainable development of the Dalit people and their communities. Given this, the differences between non-productive and productive and uses of remittances needs to be re-scrutinized in a new way. But the small proportion of remittances utilized for future saving or on other forms of productive investment such as health and education should be understood as investment in future human capital. However, the remittance receivers' ignorance of business sectors whether small or medium, failure to invest for future livelihood security, are the grave concerns.

Conclusion

Foreign employment is a vital strategy to tackle unemployment, underemployment and many other internal problems of Dalit communities in Nepal. Owing to the lack of employment opportunities and dysfunctional domestic labour market, foreign employment has been an option for the unskilled and semi-skilled Dalit labour force. Historically victimized by the state in the past, the lower educational status and the vicious cycle of caste discrimination have also forced Dalits to migrate abroad for labour. Concurring to NELM framework, Dalit households favour sending members to destinations with high earning potentials viz. Gulf countries, South Korea and Europe with the expectation of receiving higher returns. The migration of Dalit individuals has been a family-based decision, family strategy to minimize risks/uncertainties to diversify household income portfolios to protect against risk and access gain to capital in order to finance consumer and productive purchases and in return the household receive remittances for the welfare of left behind household members which is an altruistic motive. Consequently, the Dalit households received considerably higher amount of remittances from migrants who are working in countries with high earning potentials and vice versa. Such destination specific variation in the amount of remittance received by households is increasing income inequality among migrant households.

As the majority of the remittance receivers were *better consumers* of the remitted amounts, the remittance has augmented their purchasing power not only enabling them to spend on their children's education but also on other family expenditures. However, despite remittance use, there has been little improvement in their human, educational and productive assets at home. Though remittance is playing a key role in lessening caste discriminations and supporting the livelihood, the present scenario of poor educational, economic and human status, insignificant involvement in social, development and economic sectors are the proofs of inability of remittances to address Dalits livelihood problems. Remittances along with the long-term absence of family members have negative social impact such as poor emotional attachment between the migrants and their family members because of the time-gap and physical distance. Alcoholism is also contributing to familial quarrel. These entire situations are creating insecurity in Dalits lives and enlarging vulnerabilities. Remittance has increased their dependency on foreign money and is weakening economic and human assets at home. The remittance recipient families depended solely on the remitted income rather than finding alternative income generating activities at home and have failed to invest hard-earned remittances in productive works. Therefore, from the perspective of productive use of remittances, drastic changes cannot be experienced instantly despite remittance's role in changing families' livelihood. Remittance cannot reduce poverty in a sustainable manner as the socio economic condition will revert when remittance inflow stops or is limited. However, it is veracity that Dalits socioeconomic condition has improved gradually, many of their socioeconomic problems solved and relieved from financial troubles because of the remittance. But the lack of productive use of remittances by households is a grave concern.

Remittances cannot be a magic potion of development, despite its role in reducing poverty and solving many other problems of Dalit families. Though remittances are a vital pillar of Dalit livelihood, however, long-term dependence on remittance may be perilous. Also proper management of a large inflow of remittances can be precarious. While remittance income has helped reduce paucity at a faster rate and has improved standard of living, the overall self-reliant sustainable economic augmentation of Dalit has not been satisfactory. Despite remittance income being the backbone of Dalit economy, it is not a permanent solution because there has been no effort so far to develop an environment that encourages the remittance income in productive investment. The inflow of remittances should not be considered as a substitute for investment and trade. The migration of prolific youths cannot be a long-term economic and social solution to their families as well as to the country as most of the productive and enthusiastic life span are spent in foreign countries. It does not bring any social or technological changes in the village but bring changes only in consumption habit in the name of remittance triggered *consumerism* that creates heavy toll on agriculture, traditional occupations and manufacturing sectors due to labour shortage.

It is prerequisite that the remittance must be utilized in some sustainable alternative income generating productions instead of being invested heavily in consumption expenditures. Hence, the opportunities for investing remittance must be created by government and non-government sectors. Mainly, the government should motivate the remittance earners to start local enterprises based on their traditional skills for which practical policies and programs need to be developed by policy makers for encouraging the utilization of remittances for productive use in order to promote longer-term growth, sustainability and giving continuity to Dalits traditional occupations in the form of refined skill-based occupations at home. Also the formulation and effective implementation of pro-poor employment strategies and creating awareness among Dalits is the urgent need. The more there will be the investment of remittance in productive sector at home, the more will be the prospects of jobs in Nepal and in the process the trend of international migration for job will halt.

References

Adhikari, J. "Mobility and agrarian change in central Nepal", *Contributions to Nepalese Studies*. The Free Library, http:// freelibrary.com/mobility and agrarian change in central Nepal (1)-a092840368, 2001.

Agarwal, R. & Horowitz, A. W. "Are international remittances altruism or insurance? Evidence from Guyana using multiple-migrant households", *World Development,* 30:11, 2033-2044. Doi.org/10.1016 S0305-750X(02)00118-3, 2002.

Arun, T. & Ulku, H. "Determinants of remittances: The case of the South Asian community in Manchester", *Journal of Development Studies*, 47:6,894-912. Doi. org/10.1080/00220388.2010. 527951, 2011.

Central Bureau of Statistics. *National Population* and *Housing Census* (*NPHC*). Kathmandu, Nepal. Vol. 02, 2011.

Department of Women Development. *The Empowerment of Women*. Ministry of Women, Children and Social Welfare, 2003.

Government of Nepal. *Labour migration for employment: A status report for Nepal: 2013/2014*. Kathmandu, Nepal: Ministry of Labour and Employment, Department of Foreign Employment, 2014.

Gurung, H. B. *Internal and International Migration in Nepal*. Kathmandu, Nepal: HMG Population Commission, 1983.

Hay, Michael J. "A structural equations model of migration in Tunisia", *Economic Development and Cultural Change* 28: 345–358, 1980.

Hoermann, B. & Kollmair, M. "Labor migration and remittances in the Hindu Kush-Himalayan region", *ICIMOD Working Paper*. Kathmandu, Nepal, 2009.

Kollmair, M., Manandhar, S., Subedi, B. & Thieme, S. "New figures for old stories: Migration and remittances in Nepal", *Migration Letters*, 3:2, 151–160, 2006.

Lokshin, M., Bontch-Osmolovskim, M., & Glinskaya, E. "Work-related migration and poverty reduction in Nepal", *World Bank Policy Research Working Paper No. 4231*, Washington, DC: The World Bank, May 2007.

Lokshin, M., Bontch-Osmolovskim, M., & Glinskaya, E. "Work-related migration and poverty reduction in Nepal", *Review of Development Economics*, 14:2, 323–332, GRIPS Policy Research Center, 2010.

Nepal Rastra Bank Survey. *A Study on Remittance from India*. Kathmandu: Nepal Rastra Bank, 2007.

Nepal Human Development Report (NHDR). *Beyond Geography, Unlocking Human Potential.* Kathmandu, National Planning Commission, Government of Nepal and UNDP, 2014.

Sana, M. & Massey, Douglas. "Household composition, family migration and community context: Migrant remittances in four countries", *Social Science quarterly* 86: 2, 509-528, 2005.

Seddon, David, Adhikari, Jagannath and Gurung, Ganesh. *The New Lahures; Foreign Employment and Remittance Economy of Nepal.* Kathmandu, Nepal. Institute for Development Studies (NIDS), 2001.

Stark, O. *The Migration of Labor.* Oxford: Basil Blackwell, 1991.

Stark, O. & Taylor, J. E. "Migration incentives, migration types: The role of relative deprivation", *The Economic Journal* 101:408, 1163-78, 1991.

Stark, O. & Bloom, D. E. "The new economics of labor migration", *American Economic Review,* 75:2, 173–178, 1985.

Taylor, Edward, Arango, Graeme, Hugo, Ali, Kouaouci, Massey, Douglas, Adela, Pellegrino. "International migration and community development", *Population Index* 62:3, 397–418, 1996.

Taylor, Edward. "The New Economics of Labour Migration and the Role of Remittances in the Migration Process", *International Migration* 37:1, 63-88, 1999.

The Himalayan Times. *Nepal Top Remittance Economy in Proportion to GDP in Asia in 2016.* Kathmandu, 7 December 2016.

Thieme, S. & Wyss, S. "Migration patterns and remittance transfer in Nepal: A case study of Sainik Basti in Western Nepal", *International Migration,* 43:5, 59–98. Doi.org/10.1111/j.1468-2435.2005.00342.x,2005.

Wahidin, Mahamud. "Impact of Overseas Labor Migration on Bangladesh Economy: Macro and Micro Evidences: A Macro Economic Perspective" in *To the Gulf and Back: Studies on the Economic Impact of Asian Labour Migration.* Edited by R. Amjad 16-29, New Delhi: ILO/ARTEP, 1989.

World Bank. *Migration and Remittances Factbook 2016.* Third Edition. Washington, DC: The World Bank. http://siteresources.worldbank.org/ INTPROSPECTS/2016.

Zai Liang, J. L. & Ma, Z. "Migration and remittances", *Asian Population Studies,* 9:2, 124-141. http://dx.doi.org/10.1080/17441730.2013.785721, 2013.

Chapter Four

'Don't Be in a Hurry to Belong': South Asian Migration Narratives in the Midwest

Catherine Borshuk and M. Gail Hickey

Abstract

Theories or interventions about immigrant families, their cultural adaptation, and positive inter-group relations must take into account the varying experiences of migration, as well as the specifics surrounding location (place), ethnicity, class, age and gender. South Asian families arrive in the US with different socio-historical experiences and acculturation processes from those of other Asian ethnic groups. South Asians also evidence considerable diversity among themselves. This chapter seeks to advance an understanding of the identity and acculturation experiences of Asian Indian, Pakistani, and Sri Lankan groups in their respective socio-cultural contexts in the United States.

The authors address diverse aspects of South Asian immigrant identity via the scholarship on family dynamics, inter-group relations, cross-cultural psychology and educational psychology to consider such issues as: a) the impact of cultural practices and belief systems on immigrants' acculturative experiences, b) and immigrant families' experiences with formal institutions such as the US educational system. Our data set includes 90 oral history interviews with a demographic cross-section of South Asian immigrants who reside in the Midwestern United States. Long interviews covered each participant's migration narrative, as well as family and gender roles, child rearing practices, and specific cultural traditions. Emergent themes included prejudice in inter-ethnic group experiences, rationalized racism and perceived exceptionalism, leading us to conclude our participants experienced an acculturation strategy of selective integration.

How does the location where an immigrant community resides impact its members' interaction with the host culture, and its acculturative strategies? Although recent work on immigrant acculturation discusses the particularities of gender, social class, ethnicity and original culture of immigrants to the US (e.g., Sam & Berry 2006), less attention has been paid to the newer immigrant-receiving locations in the US, the small towns and Midwestern and southern places in which immigrants and their families are increasingly settling. Deaux (2006: 139) wrote that "earlier models of 'immigrant meets white host'" are inappropriate in characterizing the day-to-day experiences of many of today's immigrants who live in highly cosmopolitan settings; however, it is clear that she was talking only about those in "major gateway cities such as New York and Los Angeles". Studying the intergroup experiences of immigrants in non-traditional receiving sites can add important information to the literature on immigrant acculturation in the United States, especially as more immigrants settle in Southern and Midwestern states.

According to US Census figures, Asian Indians are one of the fastest-growing immigrant groups in the United States. Their numbers doubled just between 1990 and 2000 and continue to expand; currently, over three million first-generation immigrants from India live in the US (Chakavorty, Kapur and Singh 2017). Historically, Asian Indians have experienced similar social and legal exclusion as other Asian immigrants to the United States, beginning at least as early as 1907, when Punjabis became victims of a race riot in Washington, where local laborers were incensed that Indian men were competing for jobs in lumber mills (Helweg & Helweg 1990). The number of Indian immigrants reflects changes to US immigration policies over the past century. Racial considerations in the immigration system largely excluded Asians from immigrating to the US for much of the 20th century as the national origins quota system favored immigrants from Canada and Western Europe from the 1870s to 1965. In 1965, the Immigration and Nationality Act discarded most of the race-based restrictions on immigration, favoring instead employment-based migrants and family reunification practices (Saran 1985).

Our study examined oral history narratives of first- and second-generation Asian Indian immigrants in towns and smaller cities in Indiana, most of whom did, in fact, live the "immigrant meets white host" experience. The research allowed us to look at how cultural identities were constructed within the particular context of a non-metropolitan Midwestern US host location. The study is interdisciplinary in nature: we have used newer theories from human geography to explain an approach that seeks to understand immigrants in non-traditional locations, and we analyzed our data through the lens of social psychological research on immigrants and acculturation. We grounded our analyses in an interpretive approach that foregrounds the migration experiences and narratives of Asian Indian immigrants.

Our findings suggested that the particular locale, the class positions of the immigrants, and their intergroup contact with members of the non-metropolitan host culture led to a particular acculturation strategy that we termed *selective integration*. The participants recounted ambiguous interactions with the wider host culture; downplayed and rationalized experiences of discrimination, possibly as a coping style; and drew on self-perceived feelings of group exceptionalism to develop and maintain a selective integration style.

Acculturation and Cultural Identity of Immigrants

The field of social psychology has contributed substantially to a body of research on immigrant issues and is beginning to integrate research on social identity and cultural identity construction to its findings on immigrant acculturation (e.g, Green, Sarrasin, & Fasel 2015; Deaux 2006). Psychologist John Berry and his colleagues, who created a thoroughgoing framework for a psychology of immigration (e.g., Berry, Kim, Power, Young, & Bujaki 1989), identified acculturation as a key area for study because it deals with the direct experiences of immigrants. Acculturation is generally theorized in terms of acculturative strategies – one of four discrete styles of cultural adaptation that is dependent, to some extent, on the type of intergroup relations experienced by immigrants and members of the host culture. *Integration* is one of the styles delineated by Berry (1980) and has been identified in immigrants who desire to maintain aspects of their original culture while adopting aspects of the host culture. This style is dependent on immigrants' positive attitudes toward the original and host cultures, but also on the host culture's acceptance of immigrants. *Separation* is the style practiced by immigrants who wish to maintain most aspects of their original culture and to have primary contact with members of their own cultural group. Immigrants who do not wish to retain their original culture may end up using the *assimilation* style of acculturating, if members of the host culture allow. Lastly, if immigrants do not retain their original culture, but neither are they welcomed into the host culture, then they experience the acculturation style known as *marginalization* (Berry 1999).

While this framework of acculturation has remained dominant in social psychology, because immigrants' experiences of migration, minority status, and intergroup contact vary so widely, it has become apparent that researchers must view their acculturative strategies in light of these varying experiences (Mahalingam 2006). One important such factor for researchers to consider is locale.

Coming to Indiana: Heterolocalism

Studies on immigrant settlement geography focus on factors such as racism and labor market to examine how and where immigrants settle. Urban settlement patterns show that 60 percent of all documented immigrants in the United States live in five large metropolitan areas, and that 42 percent of New York City's and 53 percent of Los Angeles' populations are foreign-born, although only about a fifth of the entire United States population is foreign-born (Wright & Ellis 2000). Newly arrived immigrants are not the only group subject to this clustering phenomenon: in fact, most of the Midwestern United States, the area of interest in the present study, is made up of counties in which 80 - 90 percent of the population is white and native-born (Foster 2002).

Where immigrants settle, however, isn't an adequate single predictor of acculturation styles. For immigrants of color who live in non-metropolitan, mostly white areas of the United States, both region and minority status should be examined as possible factors in the acculturation process. Wright and Ellis (2000) called for research to examine individual groups of immigrants, but we contend that it also necessary to focus on specific regions of the US in which those immigrants settle, especially those that are non-metropolitan. Furthermore, acculturation needs to be studied in the context of intergroup relations, especially when members of the host society belong to a dominant racial group and the newcomers are racial minorities. Social psychology research has found that non-European immigrants to North America are at a sizable social disadvantage in terms of prejudice and discrimination due to their ethnic minority status as well as their status as immigrants (Lalonde & Cameron 1993). While such findings are valuable in a general sense, it is important for qualitative researchers to be attuned to the particularities of the community under study. For instance, although the occupational status of our Asian Indian sample reflected an advantaged socioeconomic position, at least relative to other non-white US residents, Foster (2002) reminds us that while such privilege may allow someone a measure of liberty to voluntarily construct a personal identity, it does not eliminate the pattern of racial hierarchy that still exists in the US.

Zelinksy and Lee (1998: 288) proposed the social geography theory of heterolocalism to describe newer patterns of settlement, especially for individuals of higher socioeconomic status who are more dispersed by labor markets and language skills. Their work underscored a newer pattern in which strong ethnic ties are less dependent on residential clustering: a "community without propinquity." Despite criticisms leveled at their theory for retaining assimilation as a normative and racially neutral concept (Wright & Ellis 2000: 290), they nonetheless describe our sample with some accuracy:

> ...an influx of well-educated, upwardly-striving foreigners who are now widely distributed throughout non-metro America in modest yet significant quantities. Their far-flung ranks include physicians and nurses, engineers and technicians, and business executives and managers.... Equally intriguing are the many thousands of foreign-born faculty members, not to mention students, who have become a noticeable presence on hundreds of college campuses in smaller towns as well as in major cities .

Zelinksy and Lee (1998: 290) raised questions about how such immigrants participate in ethnic identity-enhancing activities despite their geographical remoteness, and what their long-term settlement intentions are. "Only through further research can questions about these members of the upscale foreign-born non-metro population be definitively addressed". While our study is interdisciplinary rather than located solely in human geography, it does represent an attempt to answer some of these questions.

In order to demonstrate how heterolocalism is tied to our particular sample of Asian Indian immigrants, it may be helpful to present information about immigrants in Indiana, the locale under consideration. According to the 2010 Census, 29 percent of the immigrants in Indiana were born in Asia. About 6 percent of these immigrants, representing over 11,000 individuals, were born in India. Even more Asian immigrants in Indiana, 24,000, claim Asian Indian heritage. Asian Indians represent the third-largest group of immigrants currently living in Indiana. In 1960, it was estimated that 361 people born in India were living in Indiana. By 2004, there were approximately 17,000. Historically,

Indiana has not been an important immigrant-receiving state; in 1990, only 1.7 percent of the state's residents were foreign-born. However, between 1990 and 2000, the proportion of immigrants in Indiana nearly doubled, while nationally, the figure went up by 57 percent (Migration Policy Institute 2005). By 2015, close to 5 percent of the state's population was foreign born (Migration Policy Institute 2015). Indiana is now considered one of the "new destinations" for immigrants: "The southern and central regions represent the new destinations of immigrants in the United States — states where the foreign-born population grew at or above twice the national rate between 2000 and 2009" (Terrazas 2011).

Intergroup contact is another factor influenced by heterolocalism. A survey conducted by National Public Radio, the Kaiser Foundation and Kennedy School of Government in 2004 found that native-born Americans who had more contact with immigrants had more positive attitudes toward immigrants; similarly, attitudes were significantly more positive in states with a higher percentage of immigrants in the population. In 2005, only about 4 percent of Hoosiers (a nickname for Indiana residents) were foreign born - about 230,000 out of 6.3 million people (Justis 2006). About half of the foreign-born are from Latin America. One can speculate that despite changing demographics, there remain many Hoosiers who do not have regular contact with immigrants, particularly those born in India.

Intergroup contact between White residents and ethnic minority residents has been marked by a difficult racial history in the state. A town called Martinsville between Indianapolis and Bloomington developed a national and even international reputation for racial intolerance and bigotry after the long-unsolved killing of a young African American woman selling encyclopedias door-to-door in 1968 (Smith 2002). This reputation was further underscored in the wake of the 11Sept. 2001 terror attacks, when the town's assistant police chief published a widely-cited letter to the editor of the *Martinsville Reporter-Times,* which read in part: "It offends me when I have to give up prayer in school ... because it might upset Hadji Hindu or Buddy Buddha. I don't believe the founding fathers were either of these. They were Christian and believed in the one true God of the universe..." (Stuebner 2002). Martinsville may not be representative of the state of Indiana, but participants in the oral history project mentioned the town and its reputation in their interviews, and many of the participants were quite mindful of their social isolation in Middle America.

In terms of a cultural identity for the state itself, a *New York Times* article pronounced that "It is hard to run for office across this state, because there is no single Indiana" (Davey 2008 A1). The north and south parts of the state differ considerably in terms of demographics: the north is more industrial, urban, and ethnically diverse, while the south is more rural, conservative, with many counties nearly all-white. Indianapolis is in the center and has the most urban and suburban populations. In 2009, about 83 percent of the population of Indiana was non-Hispanic white, nearly 10 percent was black, 5.5 percent Hispanic, and only 1.5 percent were Asian (U.S. Census Bureau, Indiana People Quick Facts). Economically, the state has focused on agriculture and manufacturing, especially steel and pharmaceuticals.

Sample, Methodology, and Analysis

The current sample of 90 first-generation Asian Indian migrants was interviewed as part of an oral history project directed by the second author, and the transcripts of their narratives were deposited in Indiana University's Center for the Study of History and Memory. Most of the participants in the study were not part of the original group of South Asian immigrants to the US who came directly after 1965; instead, most of our sample arrived later, often as students, professionals, and spouses.

Overall, the participants interviewed were of many faiths and many languages, with the majority religions Hindu (83 percent) and Muslim (11 percent). Most were well-educated or were on their way to becoming so; 25 percent of our sample held at least a Bachelor's degree. There is a large degree of religious and linguistic diversity within the sample. For instance, while many of those interviewed in the oral history project were religious, a number were not. Although some had been born in smaller villages, most came from moderate-sized to large cities. Some families lost everything during Partition, but many were middle-class and a few reported coming from wealthy families. Overall, our participants enjoyed an advantaged socioeconomic position, with many occupying professional classes as business owners, medical professionals, and academics and had a median family income of over USD56,000. While a few came to parts of the US where family members had already settled, others were the first in their family to leave India. A few had lived in other countries before settling in Indiana, and many had earlier lived in larger US cities, allowing them to make comparisons with their present-day residence. Although a few ended up in Indiana by choice, most arrived through opportunities associated with education or job opportunities. A majority arrived in the US in the 1970s or after, when there were established ethnic communities in metropolitan areas; however, those who came directly to the Midwest reported experiencing cultural isolation.

To analyze the oral history data from these participants, we utilized a heuristic qualitative approach in which researchers use both extant theory and new data in an attempt to fully understand the phenomenon under investigation. In this regard, two qualitative researchers at Indiana University collaborated to bring different lenses through which we analyzed the vast amount of data gathered for this project. It may be of note that one of us immigrated to the US as an adult, and one is Native American.

We consider the narratives captured in this project as a cumulative case study, which is described as a "weaving and texturing" (Shank 2006: 128) together of multiple perspectives of one story – in this case, the first-person migration narrative –told by many people who share a similar experience. The common threads that carried our analysis were the immigration experiences and particularities of living in suburban and mid-sized Midwestern towns.

We performed a thematic analysis according to the constant comparative method using both open and axial coding, which is coding for main themes and for sub-categories that intersect. It cannot properly be called grounded analysis, as the oral history interviews had been completed before the collaboration began, and, therefore, one of the basic principles of grounded theory, which is concurrent data collection and data analysis (Glaser & Stauss 1967), had not been met. We analyzed for code, concept, and category. Relying on the words of Miles and Huberman (1994: 56): "Coding is analysis. To review a set of field notes, transcribed or synthesized, and to dissect them meaningfully, while keeping the relations between the parts intact, is the stuff of analysis." And although we brought the particular lenses of our respective fields of social psychology and education to the collaboration, the data themselves produced the over-arching themes.

Findings

Our analysis yielded the following themes: perceived exceptionalism on the part of participants that appeared connected to having a higher social status than native-born locals in their communities; a wide variation reported in intergroup contact with members of the host culture; rationalization, amongst some, of the discrimination and prejudice they faced as non-White newcomers; and a selective integration style of acculturation that appeared to be based on the factors just described, such as perceived exceptionalism and negative contact experiences.

Perceived Exceptionalism

Immigrant experiences with members of a host culture will always depend to some extent on the immigrants' self-perception and group self-esteem, as well as on the process of social comparison, which is a means of assessing one's accomplishments by comparing with other individuals or groups (Festinger 1954). As we noted earlier, many of the Asian Indians in our sample arrived with educational aspirations or qualifications that provided them a degree of cultural capital. Certainly, our sample of Asian Indians was, as a group, better educated and of a higher income range than the average for the state.

Not only were our participants exceptional on these points of social comparison, but they demonstrated an awareness of this exceptionalism, especially in comparison to the wider group of immigrants in the US, and particularly to the larger group of Latino immigrants. One respondent explained the discrepancy this way: "I think what happens is that you get a very select group. So, when you meet Indians here, especially people like me who come on their own, we are not average Indians. Generally, we come from very good schools... Top of our class."

Participants often referred to a sense of being an exception when they talked about intergroup contact with non-Indians. In interviews, they were all asked in a straightforward manner: Have you ever experienced any discrimination here? Typical answers were: "Not me. Others, probably, yes. But I am a [doctor, or work in a law firm, or in a university]. I am protected." One man stated directly: "I personally haven't experienced it, although I'm aware that there is racial discrimination in this society, so it may be just because of the circles that I move in that I haven't encountered it. I'm sure that if I were working in a factory or different environment I would certainly, most probably, encounter it." Given that so many participants then proceeded to describe at least one example of an apparent negative intergroup interaction with the host culture, it may be that this perceived exceptionalism aided immigrants in protecting themselves from their status as targets of prejudice.

Intergroup Contact Experiences with the Host Culture

An intergroup relations approach reflects the experiences of contact between members of different groups, taking into account particular examples or feelings of cooperation, competition, or conflict. In the case of immigration, an intergroup relations approach considers the types of encounters that immigrants have, individually and collectively, with members of the host culture, then links those contact experiences to different acculturation strategies. For our sample, this included personal friendships and relationships between the immigrants and their Indiana-born colleagues, as well as everyday casual encounters. Although many of the participants spoke warmly of their work colleagues and neighbors, it appeared that primary friendships and closer relationships were grounded in the local Asian Indian community. Much social psychology research as well as many media reports has detailed the negative response of the host culture to immigrants in the United States, especially following the terror attacks of 2001 (see for e.g., Esses, Dovidio & Hodson 2002). This hostility could certainly be a reason for Asian Indians to approach their native-born Indiana neighbors with some caution.

In the present study, there was little uniformity in accounts about contact experiences with members of the host culture, although many accounts hinted at (rather than explicitly talked about) a lack of positive contact. Other participants, however, had nothing but positive contact to report. Certainly, culturally different norms governing social life were noted by many, such as the practice of spontaneously "dropping in" on friends and family that is common in India but not as welcome in Midwestern American homes. Beyond this, some participants clearly did not see themselves as at home among the local populace. For instance, one woman said: "When my sister-in-law died [in India], it just struck me with such a shock that I would be dying here, and the thought of dying in a nursing home, away from people who are of my color, or speak my language, is a horrifying one."Another spoke of "being in exile from the homeland." Other interviews suggested that the immigrant group remained somewhat segregated from the local community, as described by one professional woman who summarized her social life this way: "Since we have enough of our own circle of friends, I think it becomes harder to mix with some of the local people also because there is so much in common with us growing up and coming here. ... And I think that is one of the reasons the locals will not mix with you either. They know that you are really comfortable with your friends." This statement is revealing in the way it suggests possible intergroup difficulties as well as a rejection of an integrationist acculturation strategy. In fact, intergroup experiences of the immigrant community did not always lead to an integrationist acculturative style; at some points, continued segregation was the strategy being considered, as reflected in this statement: "I know most Indians talk about going home [after retirement] and I don't think that's going to happen ... I read about Indian communities [here], retirement communities, where all the Indians are buying homes together, and that might be nice."

Rationalizing Discrimination

Many examples of a phenomenon well-known in social psychology as the personal-group discrimination discrepancy (Ruggiero & Taylor 1995) emerged from our data. The phenomenon describes excluding oneself as an individual from one's larger group experiences of discrimination. Several interviewees reflected this phenomenon, as for instance: "There is a certain subtle form of discrimination but I have never really experienced it personally" and "Given the fact that I speak English well, and you know, the accent is not too... The color of the skin is probably the only thing, and the fact that I wear western clothes so often when I go out probably makes it a little less. No, I can't say that I have a lot of problems with discrimination...," and "I personally haven't experienced it although I'm aware that there is racial discrimination in this society, so it may be just because of the circles that I move in that I haven't encountered it. I'm sure that if I were working in a factory or different environment I would certainly, most probably, encounter it."

Some participants reported experiencing no discrimination at all, and we wondered if it was possible that a certain amount of rationalization, in aid of ego-protection, was responsible for the denial by nonwhite immigrants of instances of racial discrimination. Or are we as researchers to take our participants at their word? Here are the first-person experiences of a university student, a social science professor, and a middle-aged banking professional, respectively: "I have kind of forgotten that I am an outsider. I feel very much that I fit in perfectly and, like, everybody's been so nice to me"; "I have never encountered any racism. I have encountered some difficulties but I never made the judgment that I am being discriminated against. I have the natural tendency to blame myself rather than the other person"; "The United States is a very decent country and most people here are very decent human beings and they have been very kind to us, they have been very gentle to us.... I never felt uncomfortable because people have been very decent and people have been very nice." As researchers who advocate for a critical transnational understanding of immigrants in a racialized context, we had many conversations about the meaning behind these sentiments.

Inevitably, some participants did report, and name, experiences of ethnic and racial discrimination; although not all used first-person language to describe the experiences, and even when experiences were described, some attempt was made to rationalize the discrimination. For example, a male interviewee explained: "... [I]n Midwestern towns such as this, even if I go and ask them something at the store, sometimes they don't follow what I say. Perhaps it's my accent. Perhaps also it's that you don't listen very carefully." Certainly, the feeling that one is not being listened to can be emotionally distancing or alienating. A woman participant expressed worry over her US-born children's future: "The discrimination factor is still there no matter where you are. I think the next generation is still going to face it, no matter, even though they don't have the accent. Even if they dropped the accent, there is still going to be discrimination." Another connected her own accounts of racial discrimination to other nonwhite Americans when describing her experiences at airports: "I get it when I'm coming in immigration ....Every time I try to go through a green light, I'm sent this way to go get my bags x-rayed. I mean that's going to happen to me. That happens to every Hispanic, it happens to every Black, it happens to me. Relentless."

Acculturative Strategy: Selective Integration

The interviews indicated that participants' acculturation styles were caught up with the post-September 11 context as well as the geographical context. One man made explicit reference to living as a racial outsider in a small southern Indiana town post 9/11: "Some people say it and I think maybe it's true, that people stare more at foreign people now. I have some friends who've put up flags in their cars or in their homes, you know, American flags or caps. I don't feel the need to do that but I do feel that we stand out a little more." Interviewees were aware that some Indians, especially Sikhs, had been attacked in the US after 9/11. One man said, "At least in the Midwest, people don't know what a Sikh is. But they don't know what a Jew is either..." This disparaging of the local environment was characteristic and may be based on class and education levels. As one educated professional said, "Sometimes you feel like you're still in the dark ages with some of the local people here."

This divergence in social class and educational accomplishment between our sample and the mainstream host culture may have been responsible for some measure of segregation between the Asian Indian professionals who were interviewed and members of the larger host culture, but it did not seem to keep immigrants entirely separate. In fact, in many towns in Indiana, according to the interviews, there did not exist a large enough cultural group to form a separate enclave. Instead, we viewed members of our sample as forging a different type of integration – a more *selective* integration – than has been described elsewhere. The enclave that existed for some members of our sample consisted of people who shared similar educational and occupational status as members of their social identity groups, for instance other members of their professional, academic or medical establishment, regardless of immigrant experiences, culture, or ethnic background. In other words, in a location where cultural pluralism is not the norm, immigrants may rely more on other aspects of the community (such as members of their occupation) for integration purposes.

For instance, a university professor noted with laughter, "Well, you know, we don't really live in Indiana, we live in this enclave part, Indiana University. I've been to the Indianapolis airport ten times more than I have been to Indianapolis." There appeared to be more identification with cosmopolitan settings than the local context, as reflected by a physician who remarked somewhat disparagingly that: "the Midwest still has to come a long way ... it takes ten years to catch up with the East coast." Clearly, some of the participants who enjoyed the positive aspects of integrating into the United States - a nation that does boast large urban centers populated with members of many cultures – but not into the local small-town life of Indiana. This is why we term the acculturative style demonstrated by the more professional participants in this research *selective integration*.

Another male professor who originally had immigrated to New York City found his first experience in Bloomington, Indiana (the home of Indiana University) jarring:

> For many people in India ... New York City represents the United States and Ireally felt very comfortable in New York City. I mean, all the throngs of people

> because you see them everywhere in Bombay and, you know, rubbing elbows on the street, commuting, getting on subway trains ... And then I took a flight to Bloomington. And then came the cultural shock. You know, I'm landing in Bloomington on a small airstrip and around me I see cows grazing. And, you know, you kind of wonder is this an airport or what. [Laughter] And, you know, initially Bloomington really was quite a cultural shock because you know, I'm used to a lot of people and used to New York which was a natural from Bombay. But, you know, Bloomington was kind of like a village.

Contrast this respondent's experience with another that demonstrates not every Indian immigrant in our study considered "the coasts" the place to be, as is evidenced by this man who had immigrated to the US some decades earlier:

> Originally, I went to New York and it was a disappointing experience because - you know, for an immigrant coming to New York it's like the Taj Mahal is sort of India for folks who are not initiated. The tall buildings of New York really are the United States for people coming to this country. So I came to New York where there's a lot of opportunities, but I couldn't take the concept of commuting as well as the crime. Felt my quality of life had suffered and then decided to collect my thoughts. I went to Milwaukee for a while.

It is quite likely that immigrants' ideas about Indiana are intertwined with their negative interactions with locals. Several parents expressed worry about the way their children were ostracized in local public schools and advised their children how to rise above petty schoolyard rejection. A woman reflected the attachment she felt for her culture in recounting this story: "I told my kids when they started school in Indiana, 'look, culture is like air. Once you are in America... you are going to breathe the air of this place, you can't bring air from India and so you are going to breathe the culture. But don't be in a hurry to belong. And don't discard things Indian just because you feel inferior.'" And a young woman recounted her burgeoning understanding of racism as a schoolgirl:

> I remember when I was in elementary school, and our whole class went on a field trip or something, and we were walking in this town in Southern Indiana. My music teacher came up to me. I happened to be walking with a friend of mine who was Black, and she came up to me and was like, you girls need to watch out, or something. And I was like, what does she mean, and realized that she was saying, this is a place where you are going to be perceived as different because you are not white.

Conclusion

In summary, our participants reported less racial discrimination in their contacts with members of the host culture than has been reported in other studies. We saw evidence of exceptionalism, of the personal-group discrimination discrepancy, and the outright denial of a racial hierarchy. Perhaps because of a self-awareness of this exceptionalism, rather than adopting a straightforward integration or separation style of acculturation, participants in the present research appeared to selectively integrate with certain members of the host culture while at other times considering continued segregation.

Patel and her colleagues (1996: 303) wrote that all immigrant acculturation is "selective, voluntary, multidimensional, and bidirectional". Adapting to a new culture, they noted, involves "a creative working out of solutions for integrating competing cultural demands" (*ibid.*). This idea both guided and was reinforced by our findings on the inter-relatedness of place and intergroup contact for Asian Indian immigrants in Indiana.

Das Gupta (1997: 588), a researcher who interviewed 2nd generation Asian Indian women in the US, wrote about cultural identity using the concept of borderlands. "'Othered' in both cultures", she wrote, her interview subjects appeared to be in the process of claiming their in-betweenness as a valid, creative cultural space where they could forge an identity ....the continual fusing of existing, apparently fixed meanings of ethnicity with interpretations contingent on the ways generations negotiate their places within cultures.

Both these ideas from the extant research, Patel et. al's "creative working out" of identity, and Das Gupta's "in-betweenness" reflect well a main finding that emerged from the present research: the process of acculturation was described and experienced in various creative and multi-dimensional ways. One of the women in our sample demonstrated how she even negotiated an in-between path between Western individualism and Asian collectivism, clearly suggesting a selective integration style:

> I think my individualism is probably very American, setting out on my own, my devotion to freedom and self development... it's not easy for me to sacrifice my self-development for family in the same way that an Indian would do. I have found myself cherishing moments alone in a way that I don't think is very Indian...

Findings from the present study suggest that while a number of participants experienced negative intergroup interactions with the host culture in Indiana, their accountings of these interactions were often ambiguous, possibly pointing to a psychological discrepancy between perceptions of their group's experience and their own personal experiences with discriminatory treatment. There was some evidence of exceptionalism among our sample as well; they pointed out the limitations of small-town Midwesterners in terms of their cosmopolitanism and understanding of different cultures and contrasted this to their own comparative worldliness. Also, while many of the participants reported feeling as if they lived in separate enclaves – not really belonging in Indiana – those enclaves were not simply reflective of ethnic or religious groups, but of class and professional social identities. All these findings must be viewed in this particular context: a relatively small group of well-educated Asian Indian newcomers, who lived in a mostly white Midwestern state, were interviewed following the 2001 terrorist attacks.

Although it is tempting to construct a general theory of all immigrants in all places, we advocate instead a turn toward the specific, toward studying particular ethnic groups who immigrate to a chosen place under specific circumstances. As Frances Cherry (1995) has argued, the "stubborn particulars" matter, no more so than when discussing migration, where researchers must contend with the stubborn particulars of place and social class. This project offered us the opportunity to understand cultural identity under a very particular set of circumstances, and that in fact may be the largest limitation of the current research: we did not compare our data or findings with those from Indian immigrants in larger and more diverse centers in the United States.

Immigration is about many things, but in a primary sense, it is about location and re-location. The place to which one relocates will inevitably influence acculturative style. To add to our understanding of immigrants' cultural identities and acculturation, we must consider the importance of race and place. These factors intersect and give rise to diverse intergroup experiences.

References

Berry, J. W. (1980). Acculturation as varieties of adaptation. In A. Padilla (Ed.), Acculturation: Theory, models, and findings (pp. 9-25). Boulder: Westview Press.

Berry, J. W. (1999). Intercultural relations in plural societies. *Canadian Psychology, 40,* 12 – 21.

Berry, J. W. (2001). A psychology of immigration. *Journal of Social Issues, 57,* 615-31.

Berry, J. W., Kim, U., Power, S., Young, M., & Bujaki, M. (1989). Acculturation attitudes in plural societies. *Applied Psychology, 38,* 185-206.

Chakavorty, S., Kapur, D., & Singh, N. (2017). *The other one percent: Indians in America.* New York, NY: Oxford University Press, 35.

Cherry, F. (1995). *The stubborn particulars of social psychology: Notes on the research process.* New York: Routledge.

Das Gupta, M. (1997). 'What is Indian about you?': A gendered, transnational approach to ethnicity. *Gender and Society, 11,* 572-596.

Davey, M. (4 May, 2008). Indiana poses a puzzle in the primary race. *New York Times,* page 1.

Esses, V.M., Dovidio, J. F., & Hodson, G. (2002). Public attitudes toward immigration in the United States and Canada in response to the 11 September 2001 "Attack on America." *Analyses of Social Issues and Public Policy, 2,* 69-85.

Deaux, K. (2006). *To Be an Immigrant.* New York: Russell Sage Foundation.

Farver, J. M., Narang, S. K., & Bhadha, B. R. (2002). East meets west: Ethnic identity, acculturation, and conflict in Asian Indian families. *Journal of Family Psychology, 16,* 338-350.

Glaser, B. G., & Strauss, A. L. 1967. *The discovery of grounded theory: Strategies for qualitative research.* New York: Aldine.

Green, E. G. T., Sarrasin, O., & Fasel, N. (2015). Immigration: Social psychological aspects. In *International Encyclopedia of the Social & Behavioral Sciences (2nd ed.),* 675–681.

Helweg, A. W., & Helweg, U. M. (1990). *An immigrant success story: East Indians in America.* C. Hurst & Co.: London

Justis, R. (2006, June). Immigration in Indiana. *In Context: Indiana's Workforce and Economy,* p. 9. Retrieved from http://www.incontext.indiana.edu/3 March2011.

Lalonde, R. N., & Cameron, J. E. (1993). An intergroup perspective on immigrant acculturation with a focus on collective strategies. *International Journal of Psychology, 28,* 57-74.

Mahalingam, R. (2006). (Ed.) *Cultural psychology of immigrants.* Mahwah, NJ: Lawrence Erlbaum.

Migration Policy Institute (2015). U.S. immigrant population by state and county: Indiana. Retrieved from http://www.migrationpolicy.org/programs/data-hub/charts/us-immigrant-population-state-and-county23 June 2017.

Miles, M.B. & Huberman, M. (1994). *An Expanded Sourcebook: Qualitative Data Analysis (2nd Ed).* Sage.

Patel, N., Power, T. B., & Bhavnagbi, N. P. (1996). Socialization, values and practices of Indian immigrant parents: Correlates of modernity and acculturation. *Child Development,* 67, 302-313.

Phinney, J. (1996). When we talk about American ethnic groups, what do we mean? *American Psychologist, 51, 918-927*

Ruggiero, K., & Taylor, D. M. (1995). Coping with discrimination: How disadvantaged group members perceive the discrimination that confronts them. *Journal of Personality and Social Psychology, 68,* 826–838.

Sam, D. L., & Berry, J. W. (Eds.) (2006). *The Cambridge Handbook of Acculturation Psychology*. Cambridge: Cambridge University Press.

Saran, P. (1985).*Asian Indian experience in the United States.* Schenkman: Cambridge, MA.

Shank, G. D (2006). Qualitative research: A personal skills approach (2nd ed.). Upper Saddle River, NJ: Prentice-Hall.

Smith, B. C. (19 May 2002). Racist reputation still haunts Martinsville. Indianapolis Star, A2.

Stuebner, S. (2002). In hate's wake: Extremists undermine a small town's efforts to overcome a legacy of racism. Southern Poverty Law Center Intelligence Report Issue 107. Retrieved from http://www.splcenter.org/get-informed/intelligence-report/browse-all-issues/2002/fall/in-hates-wake 3 March 2011.

Terrazas, A. (2011, Feb.). Immigrants in new destination states. Migration Policy Institute Report. Retrieved http://www.migrationinformation.org/USfocus/display.cfm?id=826 2 March2011.

U.S. Census Bureau American Face-Finder: Indiana (2015 update). Retrieved from https://factfinder.census.gov/faces/tableservices/jsf/pages/productview.xhtml?src=CF. Retrieved23 June 2017.

Wright, R., & Ellis, M. (2000). Race, region and the territorial politics of immigration in the US. *International Journal of Population Geography, 6,* 197-211.

Zelinsky, W., & Lee, B. A. (1998). Heterolocalism: An alternative model of the sociospatial behavior of immigrant ethnic communities. *International Journal of Population Geography, 4,* 281-298.

Chapter Five

Internal Migration in South Asia: Perspectives, Pieces and Puzzles

Kundan Mishra

Abstract

The transformation of migration from a crisis to a norm, particularly in developing countries, is at the heart of migration research. While there is mounting evidence to support, necessitate and/or encourage international migration on grounds of economic development, research on internal migration presents a more fragmented portrayal. As internal migration in South and Southeast Asia, notably in India, Bangladesh, Thailand and Vietnam- continues to draw researchers, the reliance on economic push and pull factors dominate the internal migration and the research shies away from security concerns related to internal migrants. This chapter takes a critical look at the growing interest in internal migration and leverages the concept of human security to identify some of key concerns facing the research on internal migration. The chapter addresses five dimensions of internal migration research in South Asia. First, it looks at the evolution of the interest in internal migration in South Asia. In doing so, the chapter explores the links between economic development, socio-economic inequality, and the agricultural economy. Second, it critically examines the existing- and growing- body of research on internal migration in South Asia and identifies their research focus. Third, the chapter elaborates on the need to study agency of migrants and the drawbacks of conceptualizing migration as an interaction between rural and urban economies. Fourth, the chapter evaluates human security framework to conceptualize vulnerabilities of internal migrants through an example of seasonal migrants in India and Bangladesh. Finally, the chapter concludes by identifying key areas of research for internal migration and the necessity of an interdisciplinary approach to understand its multifaceted complexities.

The transformation of migration from a crisis to a norm is at the heart of migration research, particularly in the developing countries. While there is mounting evidence to support, necessitate and/or encourage international migration on grounds of economic development, research on internal migration presents a more fragmented portrayal (Akay, 2016; Birrel & McIsaac, 2006; Cattaneo & Wolter, 2015; Green, 2006; OECD, 2011; Sin & Stillman, 2015; Smith, Helgertz, & Scott, 2016). As internal migration in South Asia continues to draw researchers, the reliance on economic push and pull factors dominate the internal migration debate and shies away from the security aspects of internal migrants. This chapter takes a critical look at the growing interest in internal migration and leverages the concept of human security to identify some of the key concerns facing the research on internal migration.

At the onset, internal migration has multiple definitions, most of them resorting to the distinction of a migrant not transcending an international border. King, Skeldon and Vullnetari (2008) emphasize that the distinction based on international borders is also questionable as some borders, like in the European Union, are more porous than others. Further, the distance traversed during migration may also not be a reliable criteria as some countries are way smaller than some of the cities in South Asian countries, for example. DeJong and Gardner (1981) define internal migration as movement between two or more communities or administrative units for a specific minimum duration, which may be contextual. Srivastava and Pandey (2017:5) note that that internal and international migration are "often distinguished from one another in terms of distance; financial costs; regulatory barriers such as immigration laws and restrictions on employment; information asymmetries; issues of integration, assimilation and alienation arising from socio-cultural and linguistic differences; and applicability of laws, including labour laws and social security provisions." They further note that the understanding of internal migration is problematized by different definitions and jurisdictions used by different countries. Thus internal migration is often characterized as inter-district, as in Nepal or Bhutan or inter-state as in India. Further, in India, the census identifies internal migration as a change in location from the place of birth which is not always accurate.

The need to study internal migration is often underlined in terms of its magnitude, complexity and contribution to economic development. (King et al., 2008) note that the earliest examples and theories of migration research were indeed about internal migration and the prominence of international migration is a more recent phenomenon. That the number of internal migrants is way larger than international migrants is observed by multiple scholars (Deshingkar & Akter, 2009; Deshingkar, Kumar, Chobey, & Kumar, 2006; King et al., 2008; Kundu and Gupta 1996; Mishra 2016; Srivastava et al., 2017; Srivastava & Sasikumar, 2003). Even in South Asia, the absolute numbers represent a huge population that moves within the political boundaries of a country. In India, the preliminary migration data from 2011 estimates the number of internal migrants to be 453 million. Considering that most of these people move due to employment related reasons, it is important to understand the motivations and drivers of individuals that decide to migrate. A higher intensity of internal migration in terms of percentage of the total population can be observed in neighboring countries of Bhutan (32.5 percent), Sri Lanka (20.2 percent) and Nepal (14.4 percent) (Srivastava and Pandey 2017).

Over the years, researchers have explored internal migration from various perspectives including, but not limited to, economic growth (Deshingkar and Akter 2009; Deshingkar et al., 2006), development induced migration (Breman 2009), climate-change induced migration (Seaman, Sawdon, Acidri & Petty 2014), livelihood distress migration (Bagchi & Kumar Singh, 2012; Keshri & Bhagat 2011) and displacement due to armed political conflicts (Maclin, Kelly, Perks, Vinck & Pham 2017). Internal migration is often studied in terms of causes and consequences of migration on the source as well as the destination of migration and its inhabitants. There is a growing body of work around impact of internal migration on source and destination markets (Akay 2016; Blau 2015), effects of state led planned relocation policies (Tjondronegoro 1991;Cunnington 2011; Kenney-Lazar 2013) and the influence of formal and informal industries on internal migration (Crepon et al. 2013), among others. This chapter, however, turns its lens towards the causes of internal migration from a human security perspective. Within that framework, it further looks for theories and empirical evidence that use decision-making process to capture the determinants of internal migration. Further, through the theories and examples of specific studies, the emphasis of the chapter is on the individual or the household.

The chapter comprises of three segments that provide an overview of internal migration research with a focus on recent research on South Asia. The first section presents the theoretical frameworks that address patterns and determinants of internal migration. This section reviews different theoretical efforts and how the understanding of internal migration has expanded in its scope from a simple wage inequality driven process to a social and human security based response to permanent or temporary threats. It also revisits the theoretical gaps that can be observed in these theories and how subsequent theories improved internal migration research when compared to their predecessors. The second section elaborates on the human security framework and its applicability towards issues of internal migration. With its focus on migrant-centred perspectives, the human security framework is extensively applied to international migration but strangely had limited application towards internal migration. This section attempts to underline the utility of human security framework in understanding the decision-making process among migrants or migrant households for a nuanced understanding of internal migration and its multiple variants. The third section presents a brief overview of recent research in South Asia on the issues on internal migration. The idea is to observe how other researchers in the region are operationalizing agent based inquiries and to seek inspiration for similar perspectives about internal migration in India.

Theories of Internal Migration

The earliest examples of systematic studies of internal migration were led by economists in the US during the 1960s. These efforts were characterised by their pursuit of a rational explanations for rural-urban migration in the context of growing urbanization and industrialization. The Harris-Todaro model (Todaro 1969, 1976), a pioneering effort that continues to inspire internal migration research, located internal migration in the wage differential between rural and agricultural economies. The model explained rural-urban migration, largely from census based data, as a process driven by economic inequality between urban and rural areas. Harris-Todaro also conceptualized migration as essentially a transfer of labour with rural areas supplying labour to meet the demands of urban areas that were being rapidly industrialized. Emphasizing migration as a rational process based on a cost-benefit approach, the model found great relevance in explaining urban growth, not only in the US but also in the Global South.

Lee (1984) also tried to explain internal migration through extensive studies in South Korea in terms of "push-pull" dynamics and a lack of equilibrium among them. A key deviation from Harris-Todaro model, however, was the attention to social and political factors including war, environmental factors and famine, for example as determinants of migration. Further, the model attributed migration to a combination of "push" factors and refrained from isolating the influence of any one of these factors on migration. In addition, the model also takes cognizance of the obstacles in the process of migration and their interaction with the push and pull factors that influences migration. Finally, migration from rural to urban areas depends on the personal factors of a migrant to support the process of migration. The portrayal of rural-urban migration as a set of economic, social and individual factors was a significant extension from the neoclassical economic models of migration and catalysed complex portrayals of migration.

Sjastaad's (1962) human capital model of migration understands migration as a process of investment. While acknowledging the economic inequality between rural and urban areas to be a driver, the cost of migration is hypothesised as a crucial factor. As Lucas (1997: 730) notes about the human capital model, "...whether an individual elects to move is influenced by the present value of the difference in income streams between alternative locations, minus any initial or subsequent, financial or psychic costs of moving." By presenting migration as a form of investment, the human capital model efficiently explained the demographic characteristics of migration, including rural-urban migration and the higher rates of migration among younger population groups. Later applications of the human capital model found socioeconomic characteristics of the migrants to be a key determinant of migration instead of just their demographic attributes. The study among migrant groups in India by Connell et al. (1976) is a notable example, where rates of migration took a U shape according to the socioeconomic characteristics among migrant groups with extremely rich and extremely poor people displaying higher rates of migration.

The later applications of the human capital model are more creative than the earlier versions and have been instrumental in exploring the complexities of migration. Notable among these complexities are the role of rent from existing capital (Stiglitz 1969, 1974), the role of information (Banerjee 1984), influence of migrant networks (Banerjee 1983, Rosenzweig and Wolpin 1985, 1988) and family dynamics within a migrant household. The following section elaborates on some of these applications and their findings with an emphasis on their contribution to the human capital model of migration. An examination of the family assets, particularly land, in the global south (Stiglitz 1974; Rosenzweig

1985; Jagannathan 1987) emphasized that the ability to rent shared assets, particularly land, in rural areas may have different effects based on different contexts. First, it may make migration beneficial for the migrant as well as his/her family members who do not migrate. Stiglitz (1974) indicated that sometimes the absence of a family member may increase the productivity of a rural family and provide the necessary funding for migration. Second, the rent from family assets may decrease the benefits of migration to the extent of making its returns negative (Jagannathan 1987). In addition, shared family assets may also motivate migrants to return. Third, in extreme cases it may increase the cost of labour in urban areas thereby restraining the economic advantage of hiring rural labour. These studies provided an illuminated understanding of family assets in rural contexts and advocated considerations of rents from shared assets, particularly agricultural land in conceptualizing migration as an investment. These studies improved the human capital model by extending the influence of these assets to the urban areas, thereby challenging the unidirectional interaction between urban and rural areas.

With the advent of behavioral economics in the 80's, the social aspects of migrant groups as determinants of sustained migratory flows gained prominence. Bannerjee's studies of migrant workers in Delhi is an illuminating example of this approach. In a key contribution, these studies turn the lens of the human capital model towards the conjugal relationships of migrants. Banerjee (1984a) found that conjugal separation is less likely among younger migrants and that permanent migrants are more likely to have families than temporary migrants. Importantly, he also finds that the likelihood of conjugal separation is inversely related to the level of education of migrants. As such, it sheds light on the role of education and family relationships in determining the nature of investment that may result in migration. In another instance, Banerjee (1991) finds low periods of unemployment among migrant workers in Delhi and indicates that this may be due to strong networks of migrant workers that help them find employment and other forms of support. The relevance of migrant workers' networks also finds empirical support in the huge number of rural migrants who come to the city without prior arrangements for employment and yet spend low periods of unemployment.

The importance of family as a unit of analysis gained further support in the formulation of migration decisions under the "new economics of labour migration (NELM)" (Shukla and Stark 1990; Stark 1991). NELM presented migration not as an individual's independent decision but as a collective mutually interdependent process, including the inter-family exchanges and the dependence of other families on migrant remittances (Stark 1991). The increased focus on interdependence in migration decisions sparked significant works on intergenerational migrants, the role of information among migrants and the relationship between skills and employment among internal migrants.

The approaches discussed above illustrate a gradual evolution in understanding issues of rural urban migration. The classical economics approaches, while still relevant in understanding systematic and "development induced migration" in rapidly developing economies, fell short on three particular questions (Muggah 2003; Kapur 2010). The conceptualization of migration in terms of a supply-demand relationship could not explain the huge number of low-skilled and unskilled rural-urban migration (Stiglitz 1974). Second, an efficient response to the scenario where an equilibrium in the wage differential is reached between rural and urban areas is reached, was evasive (Bhagwati and Srinivasan 1974). Third, it could not account for the pace of development in South Asia that continues to be way faster than in the United States or Europe. As a result, the migration flows and characteristics of internal migration are significantly different from those in the developed Western economies (Massey et al. 1993).

The human capital approach tried to address these gaps by providing insights about local contexts and integration of social determinants of migration. It has enriched the understanding of internal migration through micro studies and primary evidences that responded to questions left unanswered by macro level approaches. Another key aspect of the human capital approach was the deviation from wage differential as the dominant explanatory variable in migration. Further, the human capital approach, as evident from its diverse applications that continue to drive its evolution, expanded the scope from causal inquiries to directions of flow, uncertainties and risks in migration, behaviour of migrant communities, nature of employment and the role of families, among others. More importantly, the human capital approach has responded to the interaction between development challenges and the process of internal migration in developing economies.

Human Security and Internal Migration

In conjunction to the human capital approach, the human security approach emerged in the 1990s to formulate migration as a human security issue. Subject to an ongoing debate, the human security approach is defined in multiple ways, a detailed discussion of which can be found elsewhere (Gasper 2005; Owen 2004; Paris 2001). However, it is important to notice that the human security approach advocated the security of an individual- the human- towards "freedom from fear and freedom from wants", as the historic definition goes (UN 2009). Over a period time both "fear" and "want" have attracted diverse range of queries from political conflict, economic inequality, gender discrimination, public health and many others. Further, pioneering work by Sen (2000) presented "freedom" in terms of development and social justice which provided new direction to human security work in general and migration research in particular. However, notably a systematic application of the human security approach remains confined to international migration for two reasons. First, the emphasis on providing a complementary, if not alternative, framework to traditional security issues has limited the application to international migration. Human security and its seven security aspects- economic, food, health, environmental, personal, community and political- are often used to look at the causes and consequence of cross-border migration in terms of shared concerns, like climate change, poverty and global health crisis (UN 2009). Second, securitizing the individual (or migrant) often translates into studies of cross-border phenomenon oriented towards global policy responses. As the focus on the human in the human security approach is often interpreted as addressing internationally shared concerns, internal migration continues to be an understudied theme.

With the above mentioned limitations, human security literature on internal migration appears in three prominent themes- internal displacement, climate change vulnerability and development-induced migration. While these three themes are indeed interconnected, they are distinct in their focus on the causes and consequences of internal migration. Internal displacement often attributes movement of populations to internal armed conflicts and political insecurity (Kondylis and Mueller 2014; Deng 1999; Castles 2003). Exemplified by domestic political instability in multiple countries in the global south, the work on IDPs also includes the effect of internal displacement on the human capital of the displaced population. Climate change vulnerability, meanwhile, presents internal migration as a coping mechanism to seasonal vulnerability and its effect on livelihoods and thereby food security (Saul and McAdam 2008; Henry et al. 2004; Gray 2009). This approach has gained particular significance in multiple parts of the global south owing to the agrarian crises and rapidly increasing urbanization. As such, the focus within the later two groups is more on the causes on internal migration.

Although the thematic distinctions presented above are not comprehensive, they underline the structure-agency debate for internal migration. Agency is often conceptualized as the ability to make a choice based on one's own assessment in a situation. Structure, meanwhile, refers to the rules, resources and processes that influence the ability to make a choice as well as the quality of that choice. It is important to note that it is not a dichotomous choice between structures and agency but the nature of their interaction that is critical for an improved understanding of internal as well as international migration. As deHaas (2009:2) comments on the dichotomy of migration as a forced or voluntary response, "many migrants who move primarily for work do so because they face severe constraints on personal development at home, and the range of migration options available to them tends to be constrained and structured by economic, political, and social relations. Likewise, those who are usually characterized as forced migrants, such as refugees, exercise their agency as far as possible in the face of appalling circumstances. It is only with extreme movements such as slavery and deportation that agency may be discounted completely". More recently, internal migration in India is attributed to "uneven development under global capitalism which creates, strengthens and often destroys centers of growth" (Mishra 2016: 6).

Indeed the themes mentioned above understand migration as a result of larger processes and evade inquiries about agency of the migrant. With an underdeveloped understanding of the agency of migrant, the relationship between structures and agency in internal migration remains murky. In other words, compared to the focus on migration as a process, the attention to migrant is rarefied. The interaction between structures and agency in internal migration gains particular significance in case of development-induced migration in the global south. The decision-making process among migrants emerges in the literature as an insightful framework to study the interactions between structures and agency. De Jong et al.(1981) present the decision to migrate as a result of multiple economic and noneconomic factors by the individual in the context of the family. Further, they conceptualize the decision making to compose of two components, the choice between moving or staying and the choice of location. Importantly, decision-making being a cognitive response, includes both quantified and psychological aspects.

As Mabogunje (1970:11) notes, "The stimulus to migrate is related to the extent of the integration of rural activities into the national economy, to the degree of awareness of opportunity outside the rural area, and to the nature of the social and economic expectations held by the rural population not just for themselves but also for their children. Indeed, the notion of "aspirations" or "expectations" is central to an understanding of the ways in which the stimulus from the environment is transmitted to the individuals..." The psychological interplay also appears in whether the motivation to migrate is rooted in seeking new opportunities of protecting the existing ones (De Jong et al. 1981; Petersen 1958). Finally, migrant decision-making frameworks complement the economic rationale and human capital models of migration in two key ways. First, it contributes a psychological perspective that was missing in the characterization of migration in terms of "push-pull" factors and human capital of migrants. Second, it pays due attention to the agency of the migrant and thereby to the interaction between structures and agency. These interactions are further observed in the following section that discusses some of the key works on internal migration in the global south.

Recent Research on Internal Migration in South Asia

There is a significant body of work on migration in the global south, including historical perspectives (Hutton 1986; Bhagat 2016; Banerjee 1983, 1984a; Palmer-Jones and Sen 2003; Breman 2009, 2010; Banerjee and Duflo 2007) causes and consequences. This section, however, reviews the scholarship on internal migration in the South Asia region, particularly India, to understand the structure-agency debate better. Further, it also exemplifies the implications of pursuing structural or agent-based perspectives in migration research and the innovative ways to accommodate the two for an enriched understanding. The interest of economists during the 1970s in the development processes and the entailing population mobility is discussed earlier in this chapter. Meanwhile, the rates of migration even in fast developing economies was not high, and researchers attributed it to the characteristics of the population groups (Munshi and Rosenzweig 2009; Srivastava and Sasikumar 2003; Bhagat 2008). Particularly in India, the rates of internal migration were notably low, contradicting the economic rationale, and were attributed to low levels of social capital and practices of social exclusion (Munshi and Rosenzweig 2009).

Over the years, the low levels of social (and human) capital were traced to other structural processes of agrarian crises, uneven development and the growth of the urban sector (Sen 2000; Palmer-Jones and Sen 2003; Mishra 2016). The interplay between these three aspects is often highlighted as the root of not only low rates of internal migration but also a determinant of the characteristics of migrant population. The conceptualization of agricultural crises in terms of climate change (Palmer-Jones and Sen 2003) underline how interaction between different structures may be applied to explain internal migration. Other key examples include the role of labour laws, government policies, growth of informal sector, interaction between informal and formal sectors and social and geographic variations in economic development. Meanwhile, studies from other agricultural economies in the region like Vietnam and Bangladesh have also sought explanation of internal migration variations in structural terms, including climate change and the agrarian challenges. Mishra (2016:12) notes a telling formulation of structural influences as "...an out migrant for economic reason is more likely to be from urban areas, in the higher quintiles, from the younger age group (15-34), much less likely to be female, most likely to be in a salaried household followed by self-employed in non-agriculture or casual labour, more likely to be a Muslim or a Christian, most likely to be an OBC and least likely to be an ST, more likely to be in a low-income state or a high-income state as compared to a middle income state." The longitudinal studies by Breman (2009, 2010) on internal migrant labour in India is a telling example of how skewed development impacts marginalized agrarian communities towards distress migration.

The interaction between structures and internal migration is not unidirectional and several works have tried to capture the effect of internal migration on aspects of economic growth, for example. Studies in India and Bangladesh (Deshingkar 2006; Deshingkar and Akhter 2009) indicate that internal migration is instrumental in movement of resources and labour and plays a key role in driving economic growth, particularly in densely populated geographies. Apart from economic growth, studies have also captured how internal migration is changing urbanization in developing economies (Cerruti and Bertoncello 2003; Davis and Henderson 2003). Contrary to previous examples, these studies focus on the challenges faced by internal migrants, typically from rural areas, in urban and peri-urban locations. A key aspect of these studies is the emphasis on migration as a process resulting from structural interactions than from an evaluated and/or informed choice. De Jong and Gardner (1981) emphasize micro studies- particularly decision-making among migrants- as critical to understanding migrant behavior. They further highlight that structural explanations, while relevant in explaining broad patterns of migration must be complemented by micro studies to understand contextual variations, a thought that attracted support from other scholars as well. The empirical studies discussed below share a common focus on the migrant household as a unit of analysis and on the decision to migrate.

Emphasizing a distinction between persistent and transient poverty Gaiha and Imai (2004) underline the agency of migrants as key to effective policies. They note that "careful attention must be given to identifying sections of the rural population that are likely to be persistently poor as a result of a community-wide shock. Failure to identify them may divert resources to those suffering only from temporary misfortunes (i.e. errors of inclusion) at the expense of those likely to be poor over the long term but temporarily out of poverty due to favourable short-term circumstances (i.e. errors of exclusion). Apart from measures designed to reduce the severity of such shocks, a deeper understanding of the vulnerability of specific sections to them may also help design more effective safety nets for them" (Gaiha and Imai 2004: 262). Further studies on seasonal migration in India, Bangladesh, Thailand and Vietnam also highlight how migrants pursue migration as a seasonal shock to livelihoods, among other reasons. By doing so, the hypothesis of migrant as an agent capable of assessing (in) security and acting upon it, gains strength. Reda et al. (2012) use decision-making in migrant households to understand variances in migration to Bangkok. They find that the household assesses the access to the destination in the decision to migrate. Further, characteristics of the migrant as well as the household influence the employment quality and the improvement that results from migration. Qin (2010) also uses an agent based perspective to understand the interaction between internal migrants and the environment. The study finds that labour-migrant households have different dependency, and thus different impact, than labour non-migrant households. Bryan et al. (2014) also find empirical support for the role of initial investment in the decision to migrate during seasonal famine in Bangladesh. Through a series of experiments among communities vulnerable to seasonal famine (also known as *monga*), they find support for positive impact of seasonal migration on the migrant households, reflected by a 30 percent increase in their expenditure on food. Their experiments further show that households closer to the subsistence level income, exposed to higher risk and unfamiliar with the process and returns on migration are resistant to migration in spite of its benefits. The complexity in the decision to migrate is also supported through Thai migration data from 1985-2000 where individual preferences of the migrants had a larger influence than wage differentials, thereby explaining lower levels of migration (Shenoy 2016).

The examples above show that research on agency based perspectives towards internal migration is increasing in the region. Notably, however, similar examples and evidence about internal migration in India from migrant-centred perspectives continue to be evasive. As the body of research on internal migration in the region continues to grow, there are three prominent aspects of internal migration that do not appear as clearly in the examples mentioned above. First, the contextual variation in duration and composition of migration. In India, there are examples of internal migration, including circular and/or seasonal migration, where it may be only the individual earning male member or the entire household that migrates. The determinants of such variations in internal migration need a closer look to understand the different ways in which agency is formulated and the variance in interactions between structures and agency.

Second, scholars have often noted the low levels of internal migration in India in relative terms. Studies from Bangladesh and Thailand indicate possible directions to explain low levels of migration in India. Third, in the light of new programs focused on employment guarantee, integrated rural development, financial inclusion and vocational skills training, among others, the interactions between structure and agency need a fresh look. How do these programs influence the decision of an individual to migrate? Do these programs encourage or discourage rural-urban or urban-rural migration? How do these programs factor in the individual or household decision-making processes to determine duration or location of migration? These are some of the questions that may shape the interactions between government policies in India and internal migration as an interaction between structure and agency. Finally, as emphasized above the focus on the migrant is not advocate an isolated individualistic understanding of migration but to understand interactions between structures and agency better. While the human security framework is extensively used to understand international migration issues, its application to internal migration, particularly in developing economies is rather limited. As such, research on internal migration from a human security perspective will be a critical contribution.

Conclusion

Internal migration is a complex interplay of economic, social, cultural and personal factors. While the research on internal migration has grown over the years, the contextual variations continue to attract scholars. The theories of internal migration continue to evolve and integrate various determinants of migration and migrant behavior. While there is significant amount of work around causes and consequences of internal migration, this chapter tries to review the work around determinants of migration, their theoretical explanations, evidence from the region and recent research focus. The earlier theories of internal migration relied heavily on economic reasoning. Further, these theories were largely supported by evidence from various census data and assumed that developing economies will have the same economic growth trajectories as the Western countries. The fast paced economic growth in the wake of globalization, prompted other ways of understanding internal migration.

Over the years, as both economics and reasoning started integrating social contexts better, later theories indicated important contribution of other non-economic factors, including human capital of the migrating population, social networks, cultural values and effects of climate change, among others. These theories placed the cultural and social factors adjacent to, if not embedded in, the economic reasons of an individual to migrate. These theories were also instrumental in establishing the interactions between structures and agency in the case of internal migration. Further, driven by evidence from smaller group of migrant labour from the global south, as mentioned earlier in the chapter, these theories also provided a direction for continuous work on internal migration to capture its contextual variations and nuances.

With the advent of the human security framework, the migrant-centered perspective on migration is gaining strength. Indeed drawing from the human capital theory, the human security framework is distinct in three aspects. First, migration is characterized as a security issue and not just a socioeconomic process. With this characterization, the human security framework provides an ideal platform to conceptualize the migration as an interaction between structures and agency. Second, the focus on the vulnerabilities of the human in a given context urges a systematic exploration of the context and its operationalization in the individual. Third, the seven constituent *securities* can accommodate a wide range of issues and are focused on the migrant instead of the kind of migration. Notably, international migration research unlike internal migration research, draws heavily from the human security framework to understand the vulnerabilities of migrants. When extended to internal migration, the human security framework with its foundations not in the distinct forms of migration but in the migrant, illuminates the linkages between local, national and global issues that influence the vulnerabilities of a migrant. These linkages are evident in the studies of climate-change induced migration, arguably the most extensive application of human security framework towards internal migration.

The growing research on internal migration in South Asia also mirrors the increased interest in agent-based inquiries. Meanwhile, the understanding of internal migration in India will benefit immensely from research on decision-making in migrant households. As noted earlier in the chapter there is very little evidence from migrant households in India to pursue a discussion around determinants of internal migration. The debate so far is dominated by arguments of development induced migration and the challenges of an agricultural society. These arguments have limited utility in explaining processes of seasonal or circular migration, for example. A careful examination of migration decision-making may provide insights into how migrants assess their own vulnerability and decide to migrate or return.

References

Akay, A. (2016). Dynamics of employment assimilation. IZA Journal of Migration, 5(1), 13. https://doi.org/10.1186/s40176-016-0061-3

Bagchi, S., & Kumar Singh, M. (2012). "Distressed Seasonal Migration" In India: The "Problématique" And Paving Towards Basic Rights Of Seasonal Migrants. International Journal of Innovative Research & Development, 1(8).

Banerjee, Abhijit V., and Esther Duflo. "The economic lives of the poor." *The journal of economic perspectives* 21, no. 1 (2007): 141-167.

Banerjee, Biswajit. "The determinants of migrating with a pre-arranged job and of the initial duration of urban unemployment: an analysis based on Indian data on rural-to-urban migrants." *Journal of Development Economics* 36, no. 2 (1991): 337-351.

– "Information flow, expectations and job search: Rural-to-urban migration process in India." *Journal of Development Economics*15, no. 1-3 (1984a): 239-257.

– "Rural-to-urban migration and conjugal separation: an Indian case study." *Economic Development and Cultural Change*32, no. 4 (1984b): 767-780.

– "The role of the informal sector in the migration process: A test of probabilistic migration models and labour market segmentation for India." *Oxford Economic Papers* 35, no. 3 (1983): 399-422.

Barrios, Salvador, Luisito Bertinelli, and Eric Strobl. "Climatic change and rural–urban migration: The case of sub-Saharan Africa." ***Journal of Urban Economics*** 60, no. 3 (2006): 357-371.

Bhagat, R. B. "Nature of Migration and Its Contribution to India's Urbanization." in Deepak Mishra ***Internal Migration in Contemporary India*** (2016): 26.

– "Assessing the measurement of internal migration in India." ***Asian and Pacific Migration Journal***17, no. 1 (2008): 91-102.

Bhagwati, Jagdish N., and Thirukodikaval N. Srinivasan. "On reanalyzing the Harris-Todaro model: Policy rankings in the case of sector-specific sticky wages." The American Economic Review 64, no. 3 (1974): 502-508.

Birrel, B., & McIsaac, E. "Integrating Immigrants in Canada: Addressing Skills Diversity. From Immigration to Integration." ***Local Solutions to a Global Challenge.*** Paris: OECD Publishing (2006)

Blau, Francine D. "Immigrants and gender roles: assimilation vs. culture." ***IZA Journal of Migration*** 4, no. 1 (2015): 23.

Breman, J. (2009). The Great Transformation in the Setting of Asia. 57th Dies Natalis, (October), 18. Retrieved from http://www.iss.nl/fileadmin/ASSETS/iss/Documents/Academic_publications/breman_address _web.pdf

Bryan, Gharad, Shyamal Chowdhury, and Ahmed Mushfiq Mobarak. "Underinvestment in a profitable technology: The case of seasonal migration in Bangladesh." ***Econometrica*** 82, no. 5 (2014): 1671-1748.

Castles, Stephen. "The international politics of forced migration." ***Development*** 46, no. 3 (2003): 11-20.

Cattaneo, M., & Wolter, S. (2015). Better migrants, better PISA results: Findings from a natural experiment. IZA Journal of Migration, 4(1), 18. https://doi.org/10.1186/s40176-015-0042-y

Cerrutti, Marcela, and Rodolfo Bertoncello. "Urbanization and internal migration patterns in Latin America." ***Centro de Estudios de Población. Argentina***(2003): 1-24.

Connell, John, Biplab Dasgupta, Roy Laishley, and Michael Lipton, "***Migration from Rural Areas: The Evidence from Village Studies.***" Delhi: Oxford University Press, 1978.

Crépon, Bruno, Esther Duflo, Marc Gurgand, Roland Rathelot, and Philippe Zamora. "Do labor market policies have displacement effects? Evidence from a clustered randomized experiment." ***The quarterly journal of economics*** 128, no. 2 (2013): 531-580.

Cunnington, Paul, "Village resettlement in Laos", Vientiane: European Commission. 2011

DeHaas, Hein, "Mobility and Human Development",Research Paper, ***Human Development Reports, United National Development Program,*** April 2009

Deng, Francis M. "Guiding principles on internal displacement." *The International migration review* 33, no. 2 (1999): 484-493.

Deshingkar, P., & Akter, S. (2009). Migration and Human Development in India (Human Development Report No. 2009/13).

Deshingkar, P., Kumar, S., Chobey, H., & Kumar, D. (2006). The role of migration and remittances in promoting livelihoods in Bihar. Overseas Development ..., (December), 48. Retrieved from http://www.brlp.in/admin/Files/A Study on Bihar Migration (Full Report).pdf

Gaiha, Raghav, and Katsushi Imai*. "Vulnerability, shocks and persistence of poverty: estimates for semi-arid rural South India." ***Oxford Development Studies*** 32, no. 2 (2004): 261-281.

Gasper, Des. "Securing humanity: Situating 'human security' as concept and discourse." ***Journal of Human Development*** 6, no. 2 (2005): 221-245.

Gray, Clark L. "Environment, land, and rural out-migration in the southern Ecuadorian Andes." ***World Development*** 37, no. 2 (2009): 457-468.

Green, A. E. (2006). Routes into Employment for Refugees : A Review of Local Approachers in London. In From Immigration to Integration. Local Solutions to a Global Challenge. Paris: OECD Publishing.

Henry, Sabine, Bruno Schoumaker, and Cris Beauchemin. "The impact of rainfall on the first out-migration: A multi-level event-history analysis in Burkina Faso." ***Population & Environment*** 25, no. 5 (2004): 423-460.

Hutton, John H., "Census of India 1931: With complete survey of tribal life and system (Vol. 1), New Delhi: Gian Publishing House, 1986

Jagannathan, Vijay. "The logic of unorganized markets." Oxford University Press: Oxford (1987).

Kapur, Devesh. ***Diaspora, development, and democracy: the domestic impact of international migration from India.*** Princeton University Press, 2010.

Kenney-Lazar, M. "Shifting Cultivation in Laos: Transitions in Policy and Perspective." ***Sector Working Group-Agriculture and Rural Development (SWG-ARD)*** (2013).

Keshri, K., & Bhagat, R. B. (2011, March 8). Temporary and seasonal migration in India. Genus. https://doi.org/10.4402/genus-207

King, R., Skeldon, R., & Vullnetari, J. (2008). Internal and International Migration : Bridging the Theoretical Divide. Russell The Journal Of The Bertrand Russell Archives. https://doi.org/10.1080/1369183X.2010.489380

Kondylis, Florence, and Valerie Mueller. "Economic consequences of conflict and environmental displacement" in Shahamak Rezaei (ed.) ***International Handbook on Migration and Economic Development*** (2014): 388-424

Kundu, Amitabh, and Shalini Gupta. "Migration, urbanisation and regional inequality." ***Economic and Political Weekly*** (1996): 3391-3398.

Lee, On-Jook. ***Urban-to-rural Return Migration in Korea***. Seoul: Seoul National University Press, 1984.

Mabogunje, Akin L. "Systems approach to a theory of rural-urban migration." ***Geographical analysis*** 2, no. 1 (1970): 1-18.

Maclin, B. J., Kelly, J. T. D., Perks, R., Vinck, P., & Pham, P. (2017). Moving to the mines: Motivations of men and women for migration to artisanal and small-scale mining sites in Eastern Democratic Republic of the Congo. https://doi.org/10.1016/j.resourpol.2016.12.003

Massey, Douglas S., Joaquin Arango, Graeme Hugo, Ali Kouaouci, Adela Pellegrino, and J. Edward Taylor. "Theories of international migration: A review and appraisal." ***Population and development review*** (1993): 431-466.

Mishra, Deepak K., " Introduction: Internal Migration in Contemporary India-An Overview of Issues and Concerns" in Deepak K. Mishra (ed.), ***Internal Migration in Contemporary India***. SAGE Publications India: New Delhi, 2016.

Muggah, Robert. "A Tale of Two Solitudes: Comparing Conflict and Development-induced Internal Displacement and Involuntary Resettlement." ***International Migration*** 41, no. 5 (2003). 5-31.

Munshi, Kaivan, and Mark Rosenzweig. ***Why is mobility in India so low? Social insurance, inequality, and growth***. No. w14850. National Bureau of Economic Research, 2009.

OECD. (2011). Tackling the Policy Challenges of Migration: Regulation, Integration, Development. Paris. Retrieved from http://dx.doi.org/10.1787/9789264126398-en%0APlease

Owen, Taylor. "Human security-Conflict, critique and consensus: colloquium remarks and a proposal for a threshold-based definition." ***Security Dialogue***35, no. 3 (2004): 373-387.

Palmer-Jones, Richard, and Kunal Sen. "What has luck got to do with it? A regional analysis of poverty and agricultural growth in rural India." ***The journal of development studies*** 40, no. 1 (2003): 1-31.

Paris, Roland. "Human security: Paradigm shift or hot air?." ***International security*** 26, no. 2 (2001): 87-102.

Petersen, William. "A general typology of migration." ***American Sociological Review*** 23, no. 3 (1958): 256-266.

Qin, Hua. "Rural-to-urban labor migration, household livelihoods, and the rural environment in Chongqing Municipality, Southwest China." ***Human ecology*** 38, no. 5 (2010): 675-690.

Reda, Mulubrhan Amare, Lena Hohfeld, Somchai Jitsuchon, and Hermann Waibel. "Rural-urban migration and employment quality: A case study from Thailand.", ADB Working Paper Series No. 309, Asian Development Bank (2012).

Rosenzweig, Mark R., and Kenneth I. Wolpin. "Specific experience, household structure, and intergenerational transfers: farm family land and labor arrangements in developing countries." *The Quarterly Journal of Economics*100, no. Supplement (1985): 961-987.

"Heterogeneity, intrafamily distribution, and child health." *Journal of Human Resources* (1988): 437-461.

Rosenzweig, Mark Richard, and Oded Stark, eds. ***Handbook of population and family economics.*** Vol. 1. Gulf Professional Publishing, 1997.

Saul, Ben, and Jane McAdam. "An insecure climate for human security? Climate-induced displacement and international law." Working Paper, Sydney Centre for International Law, University of Sydney (2008). Pp 1-26

Seaman, J. A., Sawdon, G. E., Acidri, J., & Petty, C. (2014). The Household Economy Approach. Managing the impact of climate change on poverty and food security in developing countries. Climate Risk Management, 4–5, 59–68. https://doi.org/10.1016/j.crm.2014.10.001

Sen, Amartya. ***Development as Freedom.*** New Delhi: Oxford University Press, 2000.

Shenoy, Ashish. ***Migration decisions and persistent earnings differentials: Evidence from Thailand.*** Working paper, MIT, 2016.

Shukla, Vibhooti, and Oded Stark. "Policy comparisons with an agglomeration effects-augmented dual economy model." ***Journal of Urban Economics*** 27, no. 1 (1990): 1-15.

Sin, Isabelle, and Steven Stillman. "Economic liberalisation and the mobility of minority groups: evidence from Māori in New Zealand." ***IZA Journal of Migration*** 5, no. 1 (2016): 4.

Sjaastad, Larry A. "The costs and returns of human migration." ***Journal of political Economy*** 70, no. 5, Part 2 (1962): 80-93.

Smith, Christopher D., Jonas Helgertz, and Kirk Scott. "Parents' years in Sweden and children's educational performance." ***IZA Journal of Migration*** 5, no. 1 (2016): 6.

Srivastava, Ravi, and S. K. Sasikumar. "An overview of migration in India, its impacts and key issues." In ***Regional Conference on Migration, Development and Pro-Poor Policy Choices in Asia,*** pp. 22-24. 2003.

Srivastava, Ravi and Pandey, A. K. (2017). Internal and International Migration in South Asia: Drivers, Interlinkage and Policy Issues. Retrieved from https://www.

unescogym.org/wp-content/uploads/2017/06/Internal-and-International-Migration-in-South-Asia.pdf

Stiglitz, Joseph E. "Alternative theories of wage determination and unemployment in LDC's: The labor turnover model." *The Quarterly Journal of Economics* 88, no. 2 (1974): 194-227.

"Rural-urban migration, surplus labour, and the relationship between urban and rural wages." *Eastern Africa Economic Review* 1, no. 2 (1969): 1-27.

Tjondronegoro, Sediono MP. "Colonists and transmigrants in agricultural development: planned and sponsored resettlement in Indonesia." In *Migrants in Agricultural Development*, pp. 132-152. Palgrave Macmillan UK, 1991.

Todaro, Michael P. "A model of labor migration and urban unemployment in less developed countries." *The American economic review* 59, no. 1 (1969): 138-148.

"Urban job expansion, induced migration and rising unemployment: a formulation and simplified empirical test for LDCs." *Journal of Development Economics* 3, no. 3 (1976): 211-225.

Chapter Six

India-Bangladesh Migration Issue: Effects and Consequences

Shahnawaz Mantoo

Abstract

Migration, a worldwide phenomenon, has often been seen as beneficial for both the sending and receiving countries. However, post-9/11, the migration phenomenon, in general, is seen as a mixed blessing. It is also being realized that it is impossible to check illegal migration unless the sending country cooperates. In South Asia, India has been at the receiving end of the problem of illegal immigration from Bangladesh. This paper argues that such illegal migration is posing several threats, particularly to receiving countries because the issue has not been properly securitized, Neither there is a proper mechanism to deal with it. Migrants seem to have successfully bypassed legal hurdles, which has kept certain territories out of reach even for Indian nationals. If Bangladesh's internal politics and economic deprivation are major factors for this state of affairs, then permissiveness towards illegal immigration in Indian political circles is also responsible. The largely lenient political class has been prompted to take a close look at the issue as an increasing number of Bangladeshis has of late been found to be involved in anti-state activities. The paper further argues that India should formulate a proper and lucid mechanism to manage this issue but Bangladesh's cooperation too is important.

Introduction

Migration is an old phenomenon and from the antiquity, people are found to move from one place to another in search of better economic opportunities and also in search of peaceful places to avoid the oppression and political marginalization (Dalem Barman 2004: 160). Myron Weiner, a social scientist identifies five broad categories of situations where refugees or migrants are perceived as a threat to the country which produces the emigrants, to the country that receives them and to relations between sending and receiving countries. The first is when refugees and migrants are regarded as a threat or at least a thorn in relations between sending and receiving countries, a situation which arises when refugees and migrants are opposed to the regime of their home country, second is when migrants and/or refugees are perceived as a political threat or security risk to the regime of the host country; thirdly, when immigrants are seen as a cultural threat; fourthly, as a social and economic problem for the host society; and finally-a new element growing out of recent developments in the Gulf--is when the host society uses immigrants as an instrument of threat against the country of origin (Myron Weiner 1993: 15). Officially recognized as a separate category of states north-east refers to the easternmost region of India consisting of the contagious Seven Sister States. The presence of illegal Bangladeshi nationals in India remains the contentious issue that undercuts India-Bangladesh relations and is detrimental to the security of India.

Historical Background

Before its birth, Bangladesh once was an integral part of a single undivided India and constituted a part of Bengal province. Since that time People have been moving from one part of the country to the other for social, economic (trade), cultural and ethnic reasons. But this movement became a problem only after India was divided in 1947 and this part became a province of Pakistan and was known as East Bengal till 1956 and as East Pakistan from 1956 to 1971.

India shares 4,095-kilometer border with Bangladesh which is the longest among all its neighbours (Pranati Datta 2004:337). The historical, geographical, socio-economical and cultural backgrounds have caused a plethora of problems between two countries among which illegal migration is the biggest conflict (D N Bezboruah 2002: 46).

Migration from Bangladesh to India cannot be totally kept apart from that in earlier periods (Jayanta Kumar Ray 2002: 33). The problem of illegal migration at least into Assam was created by the British East India Company, who first brought the Bengali Muslim peasant from East Bengal to Brahmaputra Valley at the beginning of the 19th century" (E.N Rammohan 2006: 17) In the late nineteenth century, Bengalis became the dominant class in Assam particularly in the southern districts like Guwahati, Dibrugarh, Nogaon, Cachar, Karimganj and Hailkandi, that led to Bengali being made state language and the medium of instruction and the Assamese language was labeled as the dialect in 1937 (Ved Prakash 2007: 695).

Partition of Bengal of 1905 which took place under the British strategy of 'Divide and Rule' may be considered as one of the most important events in the context of forced migration in today's Bangladesh, though the event took place long before the emergence of Bangladesh as an independent country (Dalem Barman 2004: 161).

The second important event which led to this problem was the partition of India and birth of Pakistan in 1947. Partition and subsequent communal riots caused the massive migration of Hindus from erstwhile East Bengal (now Bangladesh) to India. In many cases, migration took place under such circumstances that immigrants had to leave the country without settling their properties (Abul Barkat 1977: 19). When the British left India, the north-east was not affected by the communal riots during the partition. However, there was uncertainty due to the influx of refugees who found themselves on the other side of the border. The north-east was suddenly surrounded by countries, each of which was competing for a share of the geopolitical space (Vivek Chadha 2005: 231). The Immigrant (Expulsion from Assam) Act 1950, was passed in the parliament which mentioned that only the people who were displaced because of civil disturbances in East Pakistan could migrate to India. The deportation of people, caused much antipathy in Pakistan, and finally, in a conciliatory gesture, the Nehru-Liaquat Ali Khan Agreement of 8 April 1950 was signed which allowed the return of those people to India who had been deported till 31 December 1950. "This led to mass exodus of the minorities both ways" (Ved Prakash 2007: 523).

The formation of Pakistan as a separate state in 1947 may be marked as the year when the population movement from East Bengal to India came under the criteria of legality and illegality. Though migration of people from this region was not new but during the period of 1947 to 1971 it occurred at a higher pace as over 4.7 million Hindus had sought refuge in India during this epoch (Pranati Datta 2004: 337).

When the Liberation War of Bangladesh began, the military of Pakistan used unprecedented force and terror to smash it which compelled about 10 million people to cross over to India in 1971. Many of such refugees returned to Bangladesh after the end of Liberation War in 1971, but a considerable undocumented segment stayed back and mixed with the mainstream of India's life (Guha Roy 2003).

Indira-Mujib Agreement of 1972

The Indira-Mujib Agreement of 1972 redefined the status of Chakma refugee in India as it declared that all those who had come before 1971 were declared non-Bangladeshis. As per the 1972 understanding between India and Bangladesh, Bangladeshi nationals who came to India after 25 March 1971 would be sent back for resettlement. The Agreement had also put illegal infiltration under three categories: (a) the person convicted by court; (b) apprehended in the process of inadvertent or deliberate crossing over and; (c) all other categories of illegal entrants, i.e. identified as such in areas far from the border and in other states of India. The Indian security side has, however, been complaining that in reality, the Bangladeshi side has been receiving the persons in category (b) only. With regard to persons in category (c), Bangladesh has been insisting on the complicated procedure of deportation through consular channels (R N P Singh 2002: 146). The Agreement legalized the illegal entrants who had committed an offence under the Indian Citizenship Act (EN Rammohan 27). The Agreement was highly resented by the natives of the north-east which resulted in a large scale agitation led by the All Assam Students Union (AASU) and All Assam Gana Sangram Parishad (AAGSP). The agitators pressurized the Assam government and Government of India to make arrangements to stop it by putting permanent barricades on the borders; detecting and deporting the foreigners out from the country; their names be deleted from the electoral rolls; the possibility of the inclusion of their names in the electoral rolls be eliminated by building up an adequate and strong election machinery; and the Indian voters in Assam be issued identity cards with photographs. Several rounds of talks between the student's union leaders and the government representatives were held with regard to the issue of detection and deportation of illegal immigrants (RNP Singh 2002: 137). The matter remained unresolved due to the differences over the cut-off year. The AASU favored the use of the National Register of Citizens of 1951 as the basis for establishing citizenship, whereas the Prime Minister insisted that 1971 be taken as a cut-off year (Vivek Chadha 2005: 240). The rebel movement in Assam was finally launched in 1979.

Illegal Migrant (Determination by Tribunal) Act

The Act came into force in 1983 and was meant to detect and deport illegal migrants through tribunals. As against the Foreign Act of 1946, this act confers upon Central Government certain powers in respect of entry of foreigners into India, their presence and departure and which is applicable to the whole country. The IMDT Act is referred as "Illegal Migration (Protection by Tribunal) Act" by Hiranmay Karlekar as it makes the determination of illegal status most difficult given the fact that illegal immigration from Bangladesh was actively promoted by important political figures in Assam. Second, the complaint against a person for being illegal immigrant could only be filed by someone who lives within a 3 km radius of the residence of the accused and that the complaint's affidavit had to be supported by that of another person who also lived within a range of 3 km from the residence of the accused. Third, the Act is applicable only to those arriving in India after 25 March 1971. Finally, the definition of the illegal immigrant was mentioned as one without being in possession of a valid passport or any other travel document or any other lawful document. This made conviction difficult because one could always claim the loss of passport, and the responsibility to prove again fell on the litigant (Hiranmay Karlekar 2005:85).

The Home Ministry informed the AASU delegation in 1980 that 9, 67,000 immigrants had entered Assam during 1961-71; 2, 14,000 were displaced in the wake of 1965 Indo-Pak War and subsequent communal riots. The breakdown of the remaining 7, 53,000 illicit immigrants were given as Hindus- 631,000; Christians 30,000; Buddhist- 65,000 and Muslims-27,000 (Ved Prakash 2007: 768). In 1974, Indian Border Security Force (BSF) detected a large number of people entering India with permits issued by the Bangladesh district authorities. The Indian High Commission in Dhaka contested the authority of the district officials to issue such permits. The Bangladesh Foreign Office dismissed such contention and mentioned that Bangladesh was allowing the return of Indian nationals who had migrated to Bangladesh under special permits (Avatar Singh 2003).

The Union Ministry of Home Affairs admits that the functioning of the IMDT Act has been "unsatisfactory", and in a presentation in mid-1999, in connection with a court case, disclosed that action under the Act had been taken as follows: Total enquiries (against suspected illegal migrants) initiated: 3,02,554; Enquiries referred to the Screening Committee: 2,96,564; Enquiry reports referred to the IMDT Tribunals: 31,264; Persons declared as illegal migrants by the IMDT Tribunals: 9,625; Number of illegal migrants expelled: 1,461 (Wasbir Hussain *The Hindu*: 176). According to Sreeradha Datta (2004: 137), "due to ethnic, linguistic, cultural, physical and social similarities, Bangladeshi nationals tend to merge easily with the local population making it impracticable to identify them."

According to Wasbir Hussian, "There is a need to make a clear distinction here, between indigenous Assamese-speaking Muslims and Bangladeshi migrants before analyzing the demographic and security implications of such population growth. Aside from Guwahati, Assam's capital (that is part of the Kamrup Metro district), the heartland of the indigenous Assamese Muslims-whose origins can be traced to the forays of the pre-Mughals in the 13th century-is located around the tea growing eastern districts of Jorhat, Golaghat, Sivasagar and Dibrugarh. In Jorhat district the Muslims comprised just 3.89 percent of the total population in 1971, rising to 4.32 percent in 1991. The growth rate was 48.04 percent between 1971 and 1991. In Sivasagar, Muslims accounted for 6.65 percent of the population in 1971, climbing to 7.63 percent in 1991; in Dibrugarh from 3.66 percent of the total population in 1971 to 4.49 percent in 1991; and in Golaghat, Muslims comprised 5.17 percent of the population in 1971, rising to 7.11 percent in 1991. It is interesting to note, in this context, that the growth rate of the Hindu population in Jorhat, Sivasagar, Dibrugarh and Golaghat was between 32 and 49 percent over the 1971-1991 periods closely comparable to the rates of growth for the indigenous Muslim population. Evidently, the Muslim growth rate in areas dominated by indigenous Assamese speaking Muslims, located far from the Bangladesh border, has been registering marginal increases, as compared to areas located close to the border (Wasbir Hussain Asian Intelligence: 2004).

According to the report of the Intelligence Bureau presented to the 38th Conference of Directors General and Inspector General of Police held in Delhi on 4-5 November 2003, there were 375,000 illegal Bangladeshis even in Delhi. The division bench of the Delhi High Court was formed comprising Chief Justice B C Patel and Justice A K Sikri, directing Delhi Police on 22 September 2003 to identify and deport 3,000 illegal Bangladeshi immigrants per month, Delhi government, however, told the court on 8 September 2004 that only 3,147 had been deported since February 2004 (*The Pioneer* 2004).

The IMDT Act could not resolve the perennial immigrant problem in the north-east. Subsequently, the Assam Accord of 1985 was conceded, which fixed the cut-off date to determine illegal migrants in Assam was 25 March 1971 the day Bangladesh was born. The Accord mentioned that all those migrants who had come and settled in the state on or before this date shall be regarded as citizens and those illegal migrants who are found to have arrived in the state after this date are to be detected and expelled in accordance with the law (*Assam Accord, South Asian Terrorist Portal*). With the signing of Assam Accord, the rebel groups launched a militant struggle against the government as they asked the government to revoke the Accord and instead enact a law that deports all illegal immigrants irrespective of their time of immigration.

In 2001, the IMDT Act was challenged in the Supreme Court by Sarbananda Sonowal, a former President of the AASU seeking a declaration that the IMDT Act was unconstitutional. It led the Supreme Court of India to set aside IMDT Act in 2005. The Court mentioned that IMDT Act "has created the biggest hurdle and is the main impediment or barrier in the identification and deportation of illegal migrants." It directed the State Government to constitute the sufficient number of tribunals under the Foreigners Act to deal with the situation effectively. The decision was seen as detrimental to the interests of millions of Bangladeshi immigrants in the country (DN Bezboruah 2006: 53).

In February 2006, the Cabinet Committee on Political Affairs, chaired by Prime Minister Manmohan Singh dropped the idea of enacting legislation in lieu of the controversial IMDT Act and decided to amend the Foreigners Act to ensure that anybody whose citizenship is in doubt gets a 'fair hearing'. In fact, it means that tribunals would be set up in Assam under the Foreigners Act 1946, as was the case when the IMDT Act was in force, to examine the veracity of complaints against suspected Bangladeshi migrants. A tribunal hearing is, however, not mandatory anywhere else. This decision by the Cabinet Committee on Political Affairs was reportedly taken after a recommendation from the Congress Government in Assam. Subsequently, the Supreme Court in December 2006 held that the Foreigners (Tribunals for Assam) Order 2006, which puts the onus of providing a person with a foreigner on the complainant as unconstitutional (D N Bezboruah 2006:53).

Implications of Illegal Immigration

The illegal immigration is one of the main reasons for the beginning of the insurgency in the northeast. The *South Asian Terrorism Portal* website has listed 38 insurgent groups in Assam. Prominent among them are the United Liberation Front of Assam (ULFA), National Democratic Front of Bodoland (NDFB), Dina Halim Daigah (DHD), United Liberation Front of Barak Valley (ULFBV), and Kamtapur Liberation Organization (KLO) (Assam Assessment 2009 *South Asia Terrorism Portal*). Many of the small groups are the offshoot of major groups. The objective of most of the groups is independence from the India which is the stumbling block for peace in the region. Most of these groups are not just terrorist groups; they are organizations, having a rigid and clear-cut philosophy and a well-coordinated system of action. According to Professor Partho Ghosh, for ULFA the illegal immigration is no more an issue. They now want independence as they feel Indian government is responsible for their economic, social and political deprivation and for a step-motherly treatment. However, their demand is irrational because even if Assam becomes independent, the population pressure of Bangladesh will engulf them in no time. They are no match to Bangladesh's demography and military. The very fact that ULFA is not even active beyond its own region shows the limited potency of ULFA (Partho Ghosh 2009).

As a matter of fact, soon after the signing of the Assam Accord, the Bangladeshi Muslims who had initially identified themselves as Assamese speaking started registering themselves as Bengali speaking. It is alleged that the political leadership has supported illegal immigration of Bangladeshi because they constitute a substantial vote bank. These immigrants were clandestinely provided with ration cards and their names were included in the voters' list. "Their ability to obtain ration cards and also to enroll themselves as voters not only gives them a backdoor entry to Indian citizenship but also provides them with a political clout that facilitates the settlement of more Bangladeshi illegal migrants in India," (R N P Singh 2002:145).

Earlier the large scale of infiltration and illegal immigration was highlighted during the Mangaldoi constituency of Darrang district by-election. As the voters' list of the constituency was updated, it was found that out of the list of 600,000 voters, objections were raised to the inclusion of 70,000 voters, on the grounds that they were foreigners. This led to the setting up of a tribunal by the then Chief Minister, Gopal Bora. The tribunal declared that 45,000 of them to be foreigners leading to the postponement of the Mangaldoi elections till the mid-term poll. This accentuated the problem and led the chief minister to direct deletion of the names of foreigners from the voters' list; however, his directions could not be implemented as his government fell on 4 September 1979 (Vivek Chadha 2007:238). Subsequent election results that have brought in considerable Muslim population in the state legislative assembly reflect the growing clout of the Bangladeshi immigrants in the political process of the region. Recently Assam's former Governor, Lt Gen. (Retd.) SK Sinha mentioned that if unabated infiltration of foreigners is allowed to continue, the situation in Assam will be worse than that of Kashmir in days to come and one should not be surprised if a Bangladeshi national manages to become the Chief Minister of the State. He was even quoted as saying that "The influx of these illegal migrants is turning these districts into a Muslim majority region. It will only be a matter of time when a demand for their merger with Bangladesh may be made" (*Economic Times*: 2009). Any attempt to delete the names of illegal immigrants from the electoral rolls and their subsequent expulsion from India raises ever louder howls in the name of "protection of minorities rights" and on humanitarian grounds. The overall Muslim population of the north-east has grown from 16 to 18 percent in 1950s and 1960s to over 40 percent now. The demographic imbalance in the north-east can be understood by comparing the annual and decadal population growth rate of India and Assam which reflects an astonishing figure (Ved Prakash 2007: 755).

However, the Muslim populations living in lower Assam, most of these immigrants are economically and educationally backward. Their children study in private Madrassas which are unregistered and which do not have a regulated curriculum. Some of these Madrassas are based on hate campaign against other religious communities (Abu Nasair Syed Ahamad 2007:191). In January 2009, the then Union Home Minister, P Chidambaram said that "I don't regard a Bangladeshi as a Muslim or a non-Muslim. He is a Bangladeshi. He has no business to come to India unless he has a visa. He has no business to work here unless he has a work permit. He is a Bangladeshi. His religion is completely irrelevant" (*The Economic Times* 2009).

Tripura has a different type of infiltration predicament. A large number floating Bangladeshi population crosses the border at daybreak for work and return home at sunset. They go for work each morning—men are mostly rickshaw-pullers, women are mainly maids and children as rag pickers-and return to Bangladesh in the evening (Ved Prakash 2007: 792). "Tripura is the only state in the North-East where the indigenous people (read 'the sons of soil') have been outnumbered after India's independence by the exogenous group. The uncontrolled post-1947 influx of Hindu migrants from East Pakistan outnumbered the tribal majority population which consequently has been declining gradually and sometime steeply from 1931 census onwards till 1981 Census. The 1991 Census proved a turning point (S Sailo 1993), because the tribal population percentage registered an increase for the first time since 1931. It rose from 5, 83,920 (28.44 percent) in 1981 to 8, 53,245 (30.95 percent) in 1991. But earlier, the reduction of tribal population from 50.09 percent in 1941 to 28.95 percent in 1971 had posed a threat to state's tribal identity"(Ved Prakash 2007:2265).

In 1999, Nagaland set up a Committee of Officials to examine the influx of suspected Bangladesh migrants into the state and devise measures to deal with it. It was formed in response to the concerns expressed by various organizations and individuals on the alarming rise of illegal immigration. Unofficial figures put the influx of such persons at over 60,000, mostly settled in and around Dimapur working as agricultural labourers in the foothills and plains area, besides doing other manual jobs. It is also noted that the State Chief Electoral Officer had directed the officials to ensure that no bogus names were included in electoral rolls during the then ongoing process of special roll revision. He also pointed out that "there has been an 'abnormal increase' of more than 3 percent in the electorate during the special revision in most of the constituencies, contrary to the national average annual increase of 2.5 percent (Ved Prakash 2007:2166).

During Oct-Nov 2001, calendars iconising Osama-bin-Laden were found in circulation in Karimganj district of Assam. Police also seized CDs and audio cassettes in Tezpur in November 2001 propagating fundamentalism. Again in November 2002, Karimganj police discovered a large number of audio cassettes containing inflammatory anti-India speeches of Moulana Dilawar Hussain Syeedi, a JEI-BD MP. Apart from the material glorifying Osama-bin-Laden, a large number of cassettes glorifying Saddam Hussein have been in circulation on both sides of the border (R N P Singh 2002:149). There are also security threats due to the rise of Islamic militancy that has started consolidating itself, particularly because Bangladeshi infiltration remains unchecked. There are a dozen Muslim extremist organizations working in the region like Muslim Liberation Tiger of Assam (MULTA), Muslim United Liberation Front of Assam (MULFA), United Muslim Liberation Front of Assam (UMLFA), Muslim Liberation Army (MLA), Muslim Security Council of Assam (MSCA), Muslim Security Force

(MSF), Muslim Tiger Force (MTF), Muslim Volunteer Force (MVF), Harkat-ul- Jehad (HUJ), Harkat-ul-Mujahideen (HUM), Islamic Liberation Army of Assam (ILAA), Islamic Sevak Sangh (ISS), Islamic United Reformation Protest of India (IURPI), Islamic Revolutionary Front (IRF), Islamic National Front (INF), United Islamic Liberation Army (UILA), United Islamic Revolutionary Army (UIRA) and Zomi Revolutionary Volunteers (ZRV). It is reported that HUM and HUJ are directly raised by ISI and thus are the most fanatical in their ideology. The purpose of these organizations is to spread radical Islam in the entire North-east.

There is also a rise of Madrassas in the border areas. According to the BSF survey, while Kolkata, the state capital and a city of 14 million, had only 131 seminaries (read madrassas) and 67 mosques, the small border town of Krishnanagar in Nadia District had 404 seminaries and 368 mosques. Many of them, particularly those recognized by the government, stick to their students, who are often from the deprived background (Hiranmay Karlekar 2005:80).

Wasbir Hussain succinctly notes that "The population explosion in Bangladesh, with 2.8 million added every year in one of the poorest and most densely populated countries in the world, creates the push factors for this silent demographic invasion. These are, however, compounded by an expansionist political ideology, implicitly or explicitly supported in the corridors of power in Bangladesh" (Wasbir Hussain 2004). The Bengalis of Bangladesh have been developing what Howard Stein calls a sense of 'psychogeography' a mental map of belonging, even though spatially they may be situated in other countries of the world (Howard F Stein 1987:147). Even pro-Indian President of Bangladesh like Sheikh Mujib-ur-Rehman had once said: "East Pakistan must have sufficient land for its huge population and Assam will give it full scope for expansion."

The Indian government has taken a number of steps including tightening of border security, deploying a large number of paramilitary forces and intensification patrolling. Efforts by Indian security agencies to push back illegal Bangladeshi migrants have been until now obstructed by erstwhile Bangladesh Rifles (BDR) (R N P Singh 2002:146). According to Partho Ghosh, "Illegal immigration is an issue we have to live with but it is important for us to manage it" (Partho Ghosh)

At the same time, there is a decline in the Hindu population in Bangladesh since the partition. There was about 31percent of Hindu population in 1947 that dropped down to 19 percent in 1961. By 1974, the Hindu population further declined to 14 percent and in 2002, it was estimated that the Hindu population in Bangladesh was only about 9percent of the total population (S K Datta 2002: 89).

According to Sreeradha Dutta, "The question of the influx of Hindu refugees from Bangladesh into India has been closely intertwined with the larger issue of illegal immigration from Bangladesh. Despite the absence of statutory regulations, it is essential to differentiate 'refugees' from 'illegal immigrants'. People who flee Bangladesh due to persecution and seek refuge in India such as Bangladeshi Hindus and Chakmas are treated as refugees. Those Bangladeshis who cross over into India seeking livelihood or economic migrants are treated as 'illegal migrant'. There is another category of Bangladeshis who commute daily to their jobs in India but do not stay over (Sreeradha Datta 2004: 138)." Thus the layered and complex issue of illegal immigrants and refugees, backed by political interests, has in fact, made the migration of Bangladeshi immigrants easier.

There are also reports that foreign agencies including the ISI of Pakistan are using this easy practice of migration from Bangladesh to set up cocoons of terrorists in India to destabilize the political systems and create instability in the country (R N P Singh 2002:142). There are a dozen extremist organizations working in the north-east and some of these are directly raised by Pakistani Inter-Service Intelligence (ISI), thus, are the most fanatical in their ideology and are maintaining anti-Indian stance. "The Army has identified villages with 'curious' population mix, in and around Siliguri that provide safe haven for the ISI operatives. Chapra is one such village, 55 km from Siliguri, with the population of 25,000, the nerve centre for illegal border trade and fake currency racket of Saudi Riyals and other currencies. There is Islampur, a town 70 km from Siliguri, with a population of 1 lakh, a known 'stronghold and hub of ISI functionaries'. The town has a skewed demographic mix: some 2,000 Pushto and Baluchi settlers from Afghanistan, engaged in money laundering and 'suspected ISI activists', 6,000 Iranians who settled here in late 1960s, all of them without any vital documents and involved in narcotics smuggling; and some Saudis who 'indulge in smuggling and other illegal activities' (Ved Prakash 2007:784).

To conclude, despite their serious demographic, economic, security and political ramifications in the north-east, these developments continue to remain substantially outside the realm of the security discourse in the country.

Bangladeshi infiltration remains unchecked and illegal immigration continues to be sensitive issue that is exploited by vested political interests. Additionally, deportation policy may seem 'un-implementable' and can be regarded as 'inhumane practice' raising international criticism, particularly when the deported population is not accepted by the Bangladeshi government which demands them to prove their Bangladeshi nationality.

Illegal migration and their settlement will remain a security challenge for India if no immediate concrete actions are taken that would involve deporting and checking illegal immigration. In fact, the deportation of the illegal Bangladeshi migrants has the potential to create a major political and communal problem particularly the people involved have the support of the politicians. This issue of illegal Bangladeshi immigrants should be taken up seriously by the security forces and the political leadership without any vested interests.

Conclusion

Illegal immigration unfettered can create security threats at the individual, national and international levels, such as exploitation of migrants, social tensions and economic and political instability. To check illegal immigration establishing and maintaining adequate border controls is imperative. However, border control has to be strong enough to stop illegal activity, but not so strong that it impedes the flow of business and other legal travelers. States need to develop legislative and administrative mechanisms that stem the flow of irregular migration. Control mechanisms must be balanced so that national security concerns do not override the human rights of the irregular migrant. BSF and Bangladesh border security personnel needs to work out strategies to deal with organized criminal activities in the border areas. Detailed population profiles of the border areas need to be created, documenting ethnicity, attitudes towards terrorist and separatist groups, levels of interaction with mainstream politics, engagement in illegal and subversive activities and attitudes towards security forces.

Illegal migrants must be denied all benefits flowing from the government, and their access to private sector employment, as well as acquisition of properties, must also be curtailed. A process of gradually disenfranchising the illegal migrants needs to be initiated. A solution to the problems of illegal migrants also needs to factor in the easy employment opportunities currently available to them. To this end, once an effective identification system is in place, employers should face strong penalties for employing illegal aliens. These measures are imperative if the flow of illegal immigrants is to be curtailed, and if the existing system of incentives for such migration is to be dismantled. Promoting the concept of Village Voluntary Forces (VVF) in the border districts and facilitating legitimate trade between the two countries will aid border security and border management. It is also important to strengthen local education, economic opportunities and training programmes and incentives must be offered to encourage people to stay in their country of origin.

Finally, social, diplomatic and military-to-military and other confidence-building measures can go a long way in stemming the institutionalization of terrorism in Bangladesh, which would have a direct effect on India's security. In order to check political and economic instability in Bangladesh, India needs to come up with proper and timely assistance. Politically, this can be done by assisting Bangladesh in state building and economically both countries can work towards establishing a free trade zone and transit facilities.

References

"Illegal immigration from Bangladesh biggest threat: Jaiswal," (2009), *Thaindian News*, http://www.thaindian.com/newsportal/uncategorized/illegal-immigration-from bangladesh-biggest-threatjaiswal100191607.html, accessed on 14/12/2009.

"United Liberation Front of Assam (ULFA)-Terrorist Group of Assam," *South Asia Terrorist Portal,* http://www.satp.org/satporgtp/countries/india/states/assam/terrorist_outfits/Ulfa.htm, accessed on 21/12/2009.

Ahmed, Abu Nasair Said, 2007, *Fundamentalism in Bangladesh: Its Impact on India*, New Akansha: Delhi

Bezboruah, D.N, 2006, "*Illegal Migration from Bangladesh*", in BB Kumar (ed.), Illegal Migration from Bangladesh, Astha Bharti, Delhi.

Bhasin, Avtar Singh, 1996, *India-Bangladesh Relations 1971-1994 Documents*, Vol.1, Siba Exim Pvt.Ltd, Delhi.

Chadha, Vivek, 2005, *Low Intensity Conflict in India*, Sage Publication: New Delhi, Thousand Oaks, London

Datta, Sreeradha, 2004, *Bangladesh a Fragile Democracy,* Shipra Publications, Delhi

Dixit, J.N, 2001, "Bordering on danger," *The Indian Express*, http://www.indianexpress.com/res/web/pIe/columnists/jndixit/20010423.html, accessed on 6/12/2008.

Gaan, Narottam, Sudhansubala Das, 2004, *Recrudescence of Violence in Indian North-eastern States: roots in environmental scarcity, induced migration from Bangladesh*, Gyan Publishing House, New Delhi

Ghosh, S K, 1993, *Unquiet Border*, Ashish Publishing House, Delhi

Gulati, Chandrika J, 2003, *Bangladesh: Liberation to Fundamentalism*, Commonwealth Publisher, New Delhi.

Jamwal, N.S, 2004, "Border Management: Dilemma of Guarding the India-Bangladesh Border", *Strategic Analysis*, Vo.28, No.1

Jayanta Kumar Ray (2002), "Migration from (East Bengal/ East Pakistan) Bangladesh to India", Dialogue, 3 (3): p. 33

Kanwa, Gurmeet, "India's Borders", *India Defense Review*, Vol.231 http://www.indiandefencereview.com/2008/10/indias-borders.html, accessed on 8/10/2008.

Karleka, Harinmay, 2005, *Bangladesh: The Next Afghanistan*, Sage Publication, New Delhi

Kiran, Raj, 2003, "India aims to deport 20 million Bangladeshis", *Independent Media Centre*, http://www.india.indymedia.org/en/2003/01/2730.shtml, accessed on 17/12/2008.

Kumar, Praveen, 2003, 'Bangladesh as India's internal security concern', *Institute of Peace and Conflict Studies,* Article no. 1255, http://www.ipcs.org/article_details.php?articleNo=1255, accessed on 11/12/2008.

Lakshman, Kanchan, "Islamist Extremist Mobilization in Bangladesh", *Terrorism Monitor Volume*: 3 Issue: 12, 17/6/2005, http://www.jamestown.org/single/?no_cache=1&tx_ttnews%5Btt_news%5D=507, 7/10/2008.

Nair, P S, 2008, *Indo-Bangladesh Relations*, APH Publishing, Ned Delhi

Paleri, Prabhakaran, 2004, *Role of the Coast Guard in the Maritime Security of India*, Knowledge World, New Delhi

Prakash, Ved, 2007, *Encyclopedia of North-East India*, Vol.2, Atlantic, New Delhi

Pranati Datta, (2005), "Effects of Undocumented Migration from Bangladesh to West Bengal: A Perception Study", Session 111, Forced migration, IUSSP XXV International Conference, France

Rammohan, E.N, 2006, *Insurgent Frontiers: Essay from the Troubled Northeast*, India Research Press, New Delhi

Singh, Avtar, 2003, *India-Bangladesh Relations: Documents 1971-2002*, Vol.1, Geetika Publishers New Delhi

Singh, R NP, 2002, *Bangladesh Decoded,* India First Foundation, New Delhi

Stein, Howard. F, 1987, *Development Time, Cultural Space: Studies in Psychography*, London University of Oklahoma Press

Tripathi, Sanjeev, 2016, "Illegal Immigration from Bangladesh to India: Toward a Comphrenssive Solution" *Carnegie India*

Ullah, Ahsan, A.K.M, 2010, *Rationalizing migration decisions: labour migrants in East and South East Asia,* Ashgate Publishing, United Kingdom

Upadhyay, Archana, 2009, *India's fragile borderlands: the dynamics of terrorism in north east India*, I. B. Taurs

Chapter Seven

Addressing the Issue of Natural Disaster as a Non-traditional Security concern in South Asia within the Human Security Perspective

Prasanta Kumar Sahu

Abstract

This paper addresses the issue of security in the light of developments that have taken place in the post-cold war scenario. It is also an attempt to explore and enlarge the field of securitization theory so as to incorporate human security within the ambit of security studies. Particularly global security after the end of the cold war has witnessed the growth of an alternative paradigm i.e. non-traditional security concerns vis-a-vis traditional security concerns at the international level. At this juncture when natural disasters are taking an increasing toll on human lives and material assets both globally and regionally it is proper to discuss the damage that disasters have on community, its security and development. The paper is an initial attempt to understand the firstly the nature of securitization theory and secondly to address the issue of natural disaster as a non-traditional security concern.

Security Theory: The Post-Cold War Response

Securitization theory has emerged as one of the most promising new approaches in the post-cold war era to the field of security studies. Unlike other approaches, securitization theory conceptualizes security not as an objective condition but rather as a process marked by the inter-subjective establishment of an existential threat with sufficient saliency to have political effects (Buzar et al.1998). In the post-cold war scenario, significant shifts have taken place with the permanent stable world order moving towards a more unstable one, the concept of security was also undergoing sea change at the same time. The term 'security' itself has become the subject of diverse interpretations both conflicting and converging.

From classical times till the end of cold war security was purely understood in terms of military – security or traditional security. Here the 'referent' point was the 'state'(Rothschild 1995). Human security has emerged as one of the prominent approaches promoting a non-traditional security concern in recent times. Here the 'human' is the referent object. Starting from the immediate post-cold war scenario when the entire world was witnessing a global showdown of the traditional security paradigm giving way to non–traditional security issues such as poverty, hunger, socioeconomic development, environmental degradation and threats, natural disasters, ethnic divisions and unrest migration and others. Here, the referent point is the 'individual' thereby making the security discourse more holistic and acceptable in the current scenario. Human Security discourse seeks to prioritize human life and dignity over state security.

Human security as an all-encompassing phrase was introduced to incorporate new emergent issues as well as socio-economic development within a framework of non-security studies to analyze the new emergent discourse in international relations. The acceptance of this concept acknowledged the withdrawal of the state from the exclusive sphere of public space and due recognition given to non-state potential threats to human life and dignity. Human security as a concept now became much more prominent in political discourse and with it the realization that absence of military /nuclear threats necessitated the exploration or fulfillment of other conditions pertaining to sustainable development and securitization of the individual or the community as the basic element of security studies.

The development of human security framework by the global human development report in 1994 of the UNDP was a pioneering step. The report shifted the focus of security from the protection of the state and its borders by military means to the protection of the individuals from a wide range of threats to their wellbeing and security. The UNHDR 1994 defined Human Security as including "safety from such chronic threats as hunger, disease and repression and protection from sudden and hurtful disruption in the patterns of daily lives, whether in homes, jobs or communities" (UNDP: 1994). This report referred to seven main categories of threats to human security: economic insecurity, food insecurity, health insecurity, personal insecurity, community and cultural insecurity, environmental insecurity and political insecurity. All these issues are quite relevant in the context of South Asia.

At this stage it is imperative to introduce the first major interpretation which has provided justification for the widening of the security studies is the 'theory of securitization' introduced by the Copenhagen School led by Barry Buzan, Weaver and others. The main contention of this school is that "threats and vulnerabilities may arise in many areas within society, but to be considered as security threats, they must be ......staged as existential threats to a referent object by a securitizing actor" (Buzan et al., 1998). For the Copenhagen School, the referent object has to be the state or other sub-state actors. The second major lead was forwarded by the 'deepening of security approach' adopted by the pluralists scholars and social constructivists,who tend to go even beyond the scope of security agenda and argue that the referent object of security should not be the state but the individual or the community of which these individuals are comprised.

The Commission on Human Security chaired by nobel laureate Amartya Sen and the former UN High Commissioner for Refugees Sadako Ogata was established to explore the concept of human security and make a recommendation for policy application. The 2003 Sen-Ogata report noted that human security complemented state security because its concerns were focused on the individual and the community which was being represented as an integral part of state security. Achieving human security, therefore, included not only protecting people but empowering to fend for themselves (Sen, 1999).

The strength and appeal of Human security are not only in its new element but in the growing inability of traditional concepts of security to generate adequate responses to many of the new causes of insecurity in the world today. The UN Secretary General Report in High-Level Panel on Threats, Challenges, and Change has greatly enhanced the notion of human security as a useful tool of analysis, explanation and policy generation. In his Report 'In Larger Freedom' the Secretary-General, Kofi Annan stated in no uncertain terms that all people have the right to security and to development. This naturally brings forward the various issues that have a direct bearing on human security so as to be discussed within a multi-dimensional perspective.

Natural disasters in South Asia: Impact on Human Development and Security

One of the major sources of human insecurity particularly for the poor and the marginalized in South Asia is embedded in the natural world originating either in the interior of the earth or in the atmosphere which is beyond the control of man. The phrase "Acts of God" encapsulates the agony of human helplessness and misery, yet the truth is that natural disasters are as much a part of the socio-economic and economic sphere as a geological and meteorological phenomenon. The priority, therefore, is to explore what constitutes security that has a direct bearing on human lives. Classical frameworks may not be totally equipped to understand contemporary security concerns. A new framework is required to explore the concerns of the post-cold war era. A disaster has become one such concern that threatens human security today.

As per the UN definition of disaster, "A disaster is a serious disruption of the functioning of the society causing widespread human, material or environmental losses which exceeds the ability of the affected society to cope on its own resources" (UNDP 2001). From 1994 to 1998 reported disaster average was 428 disaster events per year but from 1999 to 2003, this figure went up to an average of 707disaster events per year showing an increase of 60 percent from the previous year. Moreover, each year from 1991 to 2000, an average of 211 million people were killed or affected by natural disaster (World Disasters Report 2001). According to the UN 2001, alone the global economic losses due to disasters was around USD36 billion. The biggest issue was in the countries of low human development which suffered an increase of 142 percent (State of the World Report 2006). Around the world, it is the poor who face the greatest risk from disasters. Those affected by poverty are more likely to live in drought and flood-prone regions, and natural hazards are far more likely to hurt poor communities than rich ones. Ninety-five percent of the 1.3 million people killed and the 4.4 billion affected by disasters in the last two decades lived in developing countries, and fewer than two percent of global deaths from cyclones occur in countries with high levels of development.

The South Asian region is the most populous and the most hazardous continent in the world. Strikingly the data from the last decade 1995-2004 reveals that out of the total number of world occurrences of natural disasters, nearly 41 percent occurred in Asia. Similarly, out of the total number of deaths and affected people by a disaster in the world, nearly 78 percent of deaths and 91percent of affected people by a disaster are from Asia (World Disaster Report 2005). Further, within the Asian context, South Asia has a very high proportion of deaths and affected people by disasters (72 percent deaths during 1985-1994 decade). The Indian Ocean Tsunami in 2004 left 224,495 people dead accounting 90 percent of the year's death toll and affected 2.4 million people. In the same year, 69 million people in Bangladesh and India and 42 million people in China were affected by disaster (World Disaster Report 2005).

The frequency of natural disasters has increased in South Asia over than 900 events reported since 1970 alone. Between 1990 and 2008, over 750 million were affected by a natural disaster, resulting in almost 230,000 deaths and about USD45 billion in damages. In the 1970–2008 periods, floods accounted for half of the total number of events reported, while droughts counted for 2 percent but that affected more than 50 percent of the total number of population that directly suffered the losses. It is the poor communities that suffer from such hazards be it floods, cyclones, earthquakes, droughts, in this region having a significant effect on livelihood, especially for communities depending on agriculture and poor managed economy that is further affected by these calamities (World Bank Report 2009).

The vulnerability of the people in this region is further accentuated by the factor that they belong to the most populous region of the world South Asia is home to more than one-fifth of the world population. South Asian countries are significantly identifiable by a large population, high poverty, low literacy and poor indicators of human development. On the Human Development Index, India, Bangladesh , Nepal, Bhutan, Pakistan and Sri Lanka are ranked at 119, 129, 138, 134, 125 and 91 respectively (UNDP HDR 2010). Poverty is widespread especially in the rural areas of India, Bangladesh and Pakistan. Some 70 percent of the South Asian population and about 75 percent of the continent's poor live in rural areas and mostly rely on agriculture for their livelihood. South Asia is the second poorest region in the world, with 38.6 percent of the population living below the poverty line (HDR: 2006). South Asia is home to almost one quarter of the world's female population, but its share in the world's female labour force is less than 14 percent. South Asia suffers from some of the highest levels of hunger in the world, with just over one-fifth of the population not consuming the standard 2200 calories a day .While South Asia's share in the world population is 22 percent it contains more than 40 percent of the world's poor. Nearly half a billion people earn below USD1 a day, while three-fourths of the population survives on less than USD2 a day. Over 62 percent of the population is without access to basic sanitation 42 percent of the adult population is unable to read or write 55 percent of women are illiterate, and 46 percent of children under five are malnourished. Almost 50 percent of the children below five are underweight Natural resources are poorly managed in the region. South Asia does not have as much forest coverage (14.1 percent of land area) which will create great stress on the future (HDR 2006).

The present scenario creates all conditions necessary about the South Asian region as a volatile ground for natural hazards to be transformed into disasters. Disasters result from the combination of three key components: i)occurrence of natural hazards, including droughts, earthquakes, cyclones, excess rainfall, floods tsunamis, etc.; ii) exposure of people (both physically and materially) and property to these hazards and iii) vulnerability of the human and physical capital exposed due to physical, social, economic and environmental factors that increase the susceptibility of a community to the impact of a natural hazard. In South Asia, the incidence of exposure of the people to disasters is more likely to be catastrophic due to high population growth, poorly managed economy, with climate variable and change. This has led to the exposure of people and material assets to natural disaster and the inability of the states to rapidly take measures to the catastrophic event that has occurred. At present, the vulnerability factor in South Asia is very high. Due to the loss in the agricultural land, a rise in the incidence of poverty and rural poor, rapid urbanization, unplanned human settlements, unsafe building practices, and high population densities, vulnerable areas situated in the hazard zones areas, have further compounded the complex situation of hazards, exposure, and vulnerability of the region. The consequence is that disasters of every type and magnitude which occur at regular intervals, consumes lives, property, and livelihoods across the region.

This has also affected the process of economic development, particularly in the post-1990s when most of the countries of the South Asian region participated in the post- liberalization – globalization programme. Since the 1980s and the 1990s, these countries have undertaken various programmes and schemes (structural adjustment programmes) which included a combination of structural changes, reorganization and liberalization of the economy, moving from state to market economy, and increased interaction between the national and global economy. Adoption of these changes liberalized the respective economies to have a closer interaction with the global economy so as to reap the benefits of development, though globalization as a process has its own controversies benefiting the few at the expense of others. Still, a large section of the people in this region is at the receiving end of this development in spite of the rise in economic growth. Chronic poverty and underdevelopment has exposed the growing population to disasters. As the population grows the accumulated economic wealth over the years is also exposed to disaster. The damages caused by natural disasters are exerting more and more pressure on development opportunities. The government spending is placed under great stress by the repeated needs to reallocate resources away from long-term development planning and towards reconstruction activities in post-disaster events. Several state governments spend significantly more on relief and damages than on their rural development programs. For example, in the state of Maharashtra, India, a single drought in 2003 and a flood in 2005 consumed more of the state budget (USD3.5 billion) than the entire planned expenditure (USD3.04billion) on irrigation, agriculture, and rural development for the plan period of 2002-2007 (World Bank 2007). The Ocean Tsunami of 2004 affected the states bordering the Indian Ocean devastation spreading to nine states particularly impacting Sri Lanka and states of the Indian Ocean.

Disasters are not only a part of the climatic space but very much a part of the socio economic and political space. Whenever disaster strikes the question of governance comes in. But governance has always been a top-down approach in South Asia. The states still carry the baggage of their colonial past and the administrative system is still exclusionary in nature. This exclusionary administration and top down approach towards development and governance treat disasters separately from development even though disaster risk is often caused or exacerbated by mal-development or under development. Current disaster management planning and implementation focus largely on the actual disasters and recovery efforts without addressing the root causes. This approach has not helped to significantly reduce disaster risk in the past and it will not help to reduce the fast-growing hazards caused by climate change. The vulnerability if the South Asian region based on a regional study on global environmental issues by ADB which described the potential effects on natural resources as far back as 1994 had suggested strategies to avoid worst impacts. This has been also emphasized in South Asian Human Development Report 2007. A new approach is required to address disaster risk reduction in South. Asia. As argued in the South Asian Disaster Report 2008, this new approach needs to be inclusive, plural, participatory and multidimensional in nature. To address the issue of poverty, underdevelopment, mal-development, and vulnerability of a large section of the population to natural hazards a more interdependent multidimensional and holistic approach is required because none of these issues can be effectively addressed in isolation. Coordination of priorities and management of resources are the two most important criteria to deal with, which requires a balanced approach towards development that is most of the times overlooked. This situation becomes even more critical when climate change risk is added to the equation. The approach adopted by most of the states is basically a top-down development policy and planning which can certainly improve the ability of the poor and the marginalized to cope with the intensified risk of the global market and stiff competition particularly for South Asia from the global eeconomic perspective. But the bottom-up approaches must also play a vital role as it brings the people closer to empowerment and generates greater conscious about their rights and needs They can empower the people to better understand and face local risks that are no longer completely predictable due to the nature, occurrence or frequency of events of disaster. It is the poor and the marginalized who suffer the most from these natural calamities. The approach must be inclusive to address the needs of the larger section of the population. All the policies and planning for disaster response and mitigation, relief and rehabilitation must not overlook the human factor.

References

Buzan, Barry; Weaver, Ole; and Wilde, J. de (1998), *Security a New Framework of Analysis* Rutledge CO: Lynne Reiner

Rothschild, Emma (1995)," What is Security", Daedalus- Journal of the American Association for the Advancement of Sciences. 124(3): 53-98.

I P Khosla, I. P. (2003)," Evolving a theoretical perspective on Human Security", in P. R. Chari and Sonika Gupta (eds.) *Human security in South Asia: Gender, Energy, Migration and Globalization*, New Delhi, Social Science Press.

Newman, Edward (2001), "Human security and Constructivism", *International Studies Perspectives*, 12(3):239-251.

Zhijun, LIu (2006), "Contentions on the values of human security", *International Review*, 2(14).

UNDP Report (1994), UNP: New York.

Pauline, Evan(2007), "Deepening the human security debate: beyond the politics of conceptual clarification", *Politics*, 27(3):1832-189.

Sen, Amartya, (1999), *Development as Freedom*, OUP

The UN Secretary General Report (2004), *In High -Level Panel on threats, Challenges, and Change: A More Secure World: Our Sacred Responsibility*, UNP: New York.

UNDP, (2001), UNP: New York.

World Disasters Report (2001) Washington, DC

Cutter, Susan(eds.) (2005), "Environmental Risks and Disasters", Prentice Hall of India: New Delhi.

Khor, Martin (2008), "Globalization and the South: Some Critical Issues", Discussion Papers no: 147, UNTAD

World Bank Report (2007), "Climate change impacts in droughts and flood- affected case studies in India" Washington, DC

Chapter Eight

Intra-Regional Migration Practices and Rise of Anti immigrant Sentiment in South Asia

Shikha Gautam

Abstract

Borders are diminishing between countries and people are moving from one place to another for better prospect of life. South Asian continent is not an exception in the process and both intra and international migration are common phenomenon there as well. Coming specifically to intra- regional migration, the region is highly affected by the intra- regional migration trends as people from Nepal, Bhutan and Bangladesh are primarily moving to India, Afghans in Pakistan and Tibetans in Nepal either for better economic conditions or for taking refuge from unstable socio-political conditions in the source countries. With this regional shift of population, a growing tendency of discontent could be traced by the original inhabitant towards the migrants. For instance, North Eastern region of India is going through this situation due to massive illegal migrants from Bangladesh. These immigrations are not only affecting the societies but also posing questions to the economic, political and security dimensions of the region. In this sequence, it is important to understand the factors behind migration and to keep a check on illegal migration in the region. States should have proper agreements over the issues of migration and regional organization such as SAARC could be the platform. The anti- immigrant sentiments could also be minimize through the facilitation of better livelihood conditions in the destination countries which would further helpful for the migrants to mix together with the original inhabitants.

Determinants of Migration in South Asia

The movement of people from a deprived region to a satisfying place is an automatic process. This can be obstruct temporarily but cannot be stopped permanently. The South Asian continent is a highly economic heterogeneous region thus people are tend to move towards the areas of better economic compensation. Looking at the intra-regional migration trends, one can trace that people from Nepal, Bhutan, Sri Lanka and Bangladesh are primarily moving to India and Afghans in Pakistan for different prospects. These migrations are largely limited to the similar cultural belt except for the economic oriented migrants. The reasons for intra regional migration could be varied such as: 1) Natural: Floods, Tsunami, Drought, Famine 2) Economic: Livelihood opportunities, Lack of resources 3) Socio- Cultural: Poverty, Social security, Cultural affinities, Social exploitations 4) Political: Discrimination towards minority 5) Domestic Conflicts: Recent uprising of Middle East (Bharadwaj 2016).

Further as Pong Sul has elaborated that there are many factors related to out migration and it could be social, economic or political which often becomes the 'push factor' for individual or group of people. Poverty is an important factor to emigrate as it can be seen in countries like Sri Lanka, Bangladesh and Nepal (Pong Sul 2005). Migration is also seen as an important livelihood strategy in many of the poorest countries. Along with the better economic access, other common benefits are also available such as better educational opportunities, household and food availability and the access of better health services. Some of the less highlighted factors are also there such as the cross border migration because of stigma and caste discrimination which could be seen in Nepalese migration to India. Further the social influence and network across border is also one of the pull factors for migration (Sharma et al. 2015).

Climate change has also become an important push factor in the recent decades. In the South Asian continent it has impacted India, Bangladesh, Nepal and Sri Lanka in terms of migration due to vulnerable climate events. Droughts, heat waves, cyclones, rising sea level, heavy rain falls, flood strikes and landslides are often felt by two or more neighboring countries in the South Asian region. Thus migration is taking place due to crop failure, rising sea levels, flooding caused by climate change. However, if these events happen repeatedly, people will eventually forced to move to new cities or abroad to find work (Annderson et al. 2016).

Understanding the Migration Scenario in South Asia

The migration scenario in South Asia could be divided into 'within border movement' and 'cross-border movement'. The interstate movement (within border) is primarily driven by economic motivations and sometimes caused by internal displacement. The intra regional movement (cross-border) has different paradigms such as legal migration, illegal migration, refugees, forced migration, migration of deprived class and movement of criminals. Regional displacement is also an important aspect of cross border migration. According to World Migration Report (2010) of the International Migration Organization, there are more than three million internally displaced people in the region. These displaced people are becoming burden to the destination however they do not pose any security threats to the region (Bharadwaj 2016). There are various corridor of migration in South Asia which are primarily could be seen as Nepal-India, Bangladesh-India, Afghanistan-Pakistan as a result of treaties and bilateral agreements. The actual figures of these migrations are even larger than the official figures.

The migration pattern across South Asia is a multilayered process where the movement of people is highly visible on both national and international fronts. South Asian economy is primarily seen as agrarian economy but with the advent of modern world, the village folks are moving to the cities because of the limited growth and development opportunities in villages. This could be seen as a shared pattern of national and international migration where poor people choose to leave behind their home country to find better work opportunities abroad. Through these people, various industries such as construction and domestic work find a steady flow of willing, able bodied man force to fulfill their roles just to be able to send their hard earned money to their families back home (Kulkarni 2013).

In the issue of *Searchlight South Asia* it is analyzed that the cities are seen as the beckons of economy for South Asian countries which generate employments for the domestic migrants and high influx of migrants are moving to cities for better opportunities. But with the overburdened cities, low wages and unstable working opportunities inspire the workers to move to larger cities where they have better chances for the survival of themselves and their families. In Nepal Kathmandu is one such big city where the domestic rural population migrates for better life opportunities. But in an article of the Nepal daily *The Himalayan Times* in 2013 estimated that 27 percent of young Nepalese people (25-34 age group) are leaving Nepal because of weak job creation, lack of confidence in government and underemployment. In 2012 alone, 554,441 young people left Nepal in search of sustainable livelihood. If Nepal is having problems of shrunk job markets both in formal and informal sectors, it is easy to understand the thrust of people for better fortunes outside the country. Many of the Nepalese people migrate to India through the south border where they are readily take in the informal sectors (household maids, cook, drivers, delivery persons) in the cities such as Delhi, Mumbai and Kolkata, live in slum communities and send almost the entirely earned income back to their home. There are no official records about Nepali migrants in India but according to the World Migration Report in 2010, there were 1 million Nepalese living in India (*ibid.*).

Bangladesh is another country from where higher number of migrants is coming to India. Along with infrastructural boom in rural and urban India is unfolding, the cultural and social ties (linguistic and lifestyle) between the two countries and poorly fenced border between India-Bangladesh has inspired many legal and illegal migration and find relatively lucrative jobs (Bhardwaj 2016). There are 2 crore illegal Bangladeshi migrants are living in India according to the Government of India report in 2016. Foreign migrants are not only limited to the household work and manual laborers but sometimes they cross the border for being financially independent (especially female migrants) and to achieve this they usually end up working as prostitutes and sex workers. Men are however in majority when it comes to gender proportion in migrant workers as it is estimated that only 30,000 women migrants are registered which less than 5 percent of total outflow of workers as is reported by *Government of Bangladesh's Bureau of Manpower Employment and Training (BMet)* (*ibid.*).

There are also a significant number of Pakistani migrations in India but it is majorly cultural migration than economic because of the social ties between India and Pakistan. Besides this terrorism is also a form of illegal migration from Pakistan. Along with this India receives significant migrations from Sri Lanka and Bhutan to some extent.

Pakistan is another country which has the second largest protracted refugee population with 1.5 million Proof of Residency (PoR) card holders according to United Nations High Commissioner for Refugees (UNHCR) mandate in 2015. In addition, 1 million undocumented Afghans were also living in Pakistan, according to the Pakistani officials. The migration of Afghans to Pakistan has various stages though the major influx happened in the period of 1970s and 80s, because of the war with the Soviet Union. The then, Pakistani government and United States as its ally considered this migration useful to their interest as some of them provided resources and manpower against the Soviet influence on Afghanistan. These migrants were mainly limited to the NWFP and Baluchistan where they have cultural affinities. Most of them employed in construction sites and opened restaurants in Peshawar and Quetta. They adopted Urdu through education and intermarriages but with the end of cold war and demise of communism, the Afghans in Pakistan began to experience hostility from the government (Human Rights Watch 2016).

Further with the emergence of Taliban in Afghanistan and the negative response from international community made Pakistan to sought a distance from Afghanistan and its people. The so called 'war on terror' project made Pakistanis to position themselves as good Muslims in the juxtaposition of Afghans as bad Muslims. With the deteriorating situation in Afghanistan, the flow of refugees increased thus the government of Pakistan decided to close the borders with Afghanistan and refused to take any further admission of refugees. However, in 2006 Pakistan began a registration camp through which about 1 million Afghan were registered and provided a proof of identity for a period of 3 years but it has extended to 31st Dec. 2017 (Abraham 2013).

Migration: Challenges and Opportunities

Migration from one place to another became an inevitable phenomenon where people often cross the border in search of better life conditions. But the process confronts various issues at both (source and destination) ends. These issues can be divided into four sections: a) the types of migration happening in South Asian continent and how it is impacting on source and destination countries. b) the struggles and vulnerabilities migrants are going through. c) Anti- immigrant sentiments and role of state to combat it.

Migration, Labour and Remittances

Looking at the wider prospect of migration i.e. at the national front, migration helps to prosper economy at both ends as it provide labor force to the destination countries and helps the economy of home country as well through remittances. But in the South Asian continent the scenario is different because of the nature of economy. Countries like India and Pakistan are developing economies with exploding population and insufficient opportunities. And with this background, the arrival of migrants (especially semi skilled and unskilled) can only cause trouble.

In the source countries, migration contributes significantly to the families and national economies as well through remittances. In 2005 estimates of south- south remittances ranged from 9 to 30 percent of developing countries remittances receipt. In Bangladesh and Nepal, remittances are larger than the national foreign exchange. For Bangladesh's economy, remittances constitute almost one- third of foreign exchange earnings. However due to the increase of unskilled and semi skilled labours, remittances are increasing at much lower rate than the labour flow. Remittances are also very important to the economy of Nepal and it is estimated that nearly 20 percent of its GDP in 2010-11constitutes of remittances sent by Nepalese migrant workers from abroad. Remittances are a major source of income for the household earning as it provide the daily needs and is a lifeline by paying education, buying land for farming, building home and investing in business. The family expects the migrant to improve their well being and health but a study conducted in Indonesia shows that despite earning a high income, migrants tend to under-consume and remit a large amount of earning to families at the place of origin which hinders migrants own health and potential gains (Sharma et al. 2015).

Migrants: Vulnerabilities and Exploitation

The effects of migration are not limited to the macro level but it has its impact on micro or individual level as well. The issues confronting by migrants can be divided into two categories first, at the stage of recruitment and second, in destination countries or workplace. In the South Asian continent where a significant number of migrants are coming from semi skilled and unskilled labourer group, they are struggling with the mal-practice of recruitment process, insufficient discriminatory wages, poor living conditions and work quality in compare to non- migrant workers. Further discriminatory practices are being practiced by government officials as well such as delays in issuing beneficiary card, differential access to the government supported food security and health facilities. Migrants who have been moved to different socio-cultural destination may face language barriers, engage in risky work conditions and harassment and unable (sometimes unwilling) to access public services due to restrictive and reactionary behavior of government staff. These life conditions may cause loneliness and depression. In a research conducted by Asia Foundation in 2013 found that there are several kind of exploitation migrants have to face in the destination country such as being scolded and battered by the owner or manager

(19.2 percent) sexual harassment by the owner (3.8 percent), owner threatening to kill them (3.8 percent) were reported by Nepali female migrants. Further the report has shown that there are serious cases of violence and harassment against the Nepalese migrants in India which leads to human rights violence at different level at the time of migration and highlighted the role of middleman and brokers into it (*ibid.*).

Trafficking and illegal migration is an important aspect of this discourse. Many trafficked individual consent to individual to the initial movement through a facilitator and it only becomes evident at their destination that they have been deceived and are being exploited. Amnest International's research conducted in 2011 also found that some recruitment agencies and brokers are involved in the trafficking and exploitation of Nepalese women in India (*ibid.*). The trafficked and irregular migrants have to face additional costs and vulnerabilities. Studies have shown that Nepalese and Bangladeshi migrants are employed at the low end of labour market especially in the service sector. The major issue related to cross border migration is irregular migration and human trafficking. Irregular and undocumented migration, particularly which is treated as illegal migration is the main concern of South Asian countries. Brokers and middleman plays an important role in illegal migration where women have to suffer more than the male counterpart. Intra-regional migration circuits in South Asia lead to significant human trafficking and countries in the region are the origin and transit as well as destination of trafficked women and bonded labourers (Srivastava and Pandey 2017). Exploitation of migrants in the destination countries is usually seen as failure of these countries to recognize the human rights.

There are varied effects of migratory practices as it affects health of the migrants as well. The national and international migration has different implications on the health of different migrant groups. Also the disease patterns are influenced by the environment of origin and destination countries and by the process of migration itself. Climate change, economic necessity and global conflicts are the driving forces behind the massive migration. The sheer scale of displacement and migration has turned migrant health into global public health issue because of the high potential of the spread of infectious disease that the mobile population brings with them. To prioritize migrant health, World Health Orgnization (WHO) in 2008 has called upon its member states to draft and promote migrant sensitive health policies, equitable access to health promotion, and disease prevention health programmes for them (*ibid.*).

Anti-immigrant Sentiments, Security and Response from the State

The history of world revolves around migration and migration has taken place since the evolution of human being and this process impacted the political, social, economic fabric of the destination. It impacts the receiving country in both positive and negative ways. On the one hand, migration has enriched the cultural, social, economic aspects of the destination countries but their prosperity has fuelled resentment among the locals. This intense resentment resulted into competition for the resources between local and the migrants. The tension between them become greater when it gets politicized and demands for the preservation of local identity which in turn has fuelled to the political disturbance and violence which in turn harm the internal security of the country. Consequently, migration is regarded as a threat to the political and social integration of the receiving country and therefore considered as security risk. Countries are trying to tighten the border control through imposing restrictive measures towards migration.

India is seen as a country of migrants since it has received people from all over the world and from different culture which provided a composite culture. While enriching the land, introducing new industry and machinery, paradoxically immigration has been a source of conflict as well. In the contemporary times, India has received a significant number of migrations from its neighbouring countries. While some of these immigrants are fleeing to India due to political and religious repressions, others are economic migrants who are just escaping from the poverty and bleak future back home. India has been hosting these migrants from a long time but the undocumented illegal migrations from Bangladesh are becoming a source of conflict in the receiving states such as Assam, West Bengal and Tripura.

The tussle between the native Assamese and immigrants Bengali was started in the 1960s where it begun over the issues of government jobs (a significant number of Hindu Bengali migrant have monopolized the government jobs) and imposition of Bengali language over Assamese as official language. The communities clashed with each other over the issue of language since 1960s. The natives feared that the cultural identity will be compromised thus they opposed the migration and demanded new state within Assam. The decline in Assamese population in the region between 1961-71, in the census increased the anxieties. The All Assamese Student Union (AASU) and All Aasam Gana Sangram

Parishad (AAGSP) started a statewide agitation against the migrant movement in Assam in 1979. This agitation spread over the North Eastern states along with Manipur, Meghalaya and Tripura where Bengali, Nepali and Bihari were attacked on the name of foreigners and other associations have formed National Liberation Front of Tripura (NLFT) and All Tripura Tiger Force (ATTF) in 1989 against the migrants. In 2014, this agitation again fuelled up against the Muslims perceived as illegal migrants (Das 2016).

There is also a security dynamics which appears with the coming of migrants to a country. When it comes to Bangladeshi immigrants in India, the illegal immigration needs a check as the impact of illegal Bangladeshi immigration could be seen in two ways. First, conflict over resources, economic opportunities, cultural dominance, and political instability through the popular perception against the migrants by the elites to grab power. Second, the rule of the law and integrity of the country are threatened by the illegal migrants who are engaged in illegal or anti-national activities such as acquiring identity card fraudulently, exercise voting rights in India despite having Bangladeshi identity, indulge in trans border smuggling and other crimes. There are many instances of radicalization of the certain section of migrant Muslims with the formation of various militant organizations such as Muslim United Liberation Tiger of Assam (MULTA) and the Muslim United Liberation Front of Assam (MULFA), asserting Jihad against India to avenge the attacks. The arrest of some of the MULTA cadre revealed that they had received training from Al- Qaeda and Taliban. They have close links with the Pakistan Inter- Services Intelligence (ISI) and other sunni radical groups such as Sipah- i- Sabaha Pakistan (SSP) and HUJI. These activities signify that the illegal migrants are posing an internal security threat (ibid).

The scenario of Afghans in Pakistan is although different as Afghan migration in Pakistan was encouraged in the period of 1970s- 90s to satisfy the interests by the then Pakistan government but in the present time the migrants are countering discrimination and harassment from the government officials as they are facing forced mass deportation. Also they have to face physical and mental abuse and daily tortures through mass arrest and search operations. In an instance, a man who was living in Pakistan from 1982 was arrested and asked to give 20,000 rupees as a bribe to the police. Those who have deported to Afghanistan have no option but to come back to Pakistan because of the poor opportunities and violence. Only registered Afghans with valid proof of registration card (PoR) are considered legal in Pakistan. For those who are living without the identity card has to get scrutinized everywhere and after the launch of 'war on terror', they always have the fear of getting arrested. Further, the deteriorating Pakistan-Afghanistan relations could also be one of the reasons for anti- immigrant sentiments which resulted in targeted harassment of Afghans in Pakistan (Alimia 2012).

Looking at both the cases in India and Pakistan, the causes of anti immigrant sentiments among the natives are clear. Now it is important to look at the response of state towards the issue. The role of state could be seen in two ways. One, it is important to implement mechanism to keep a check on illegal cross border immigration along with the scrutiny over threatening elements in the state two, protection of immigrants' rights. In this context, the Indian state, it has undertaken various measures to combat the issue of migrants such as legislations for addressing Land Alienation (1974) among the tribal's of Tripura which was for the people who are displaced by floods and earthquakes but it benefited the Bengali migrants instead of the tribal and hence it has been proved ineffective. Further the schemes of detention and deportation of illegal migrants called as Illegal Migrants (Determination by Tribunal Act 1983) yield some success and the Bhartiya Janta Party has played a significant role in the forcible deportation of illegal migrants under the 'Push Back Operation' because of the adverse effects of illegal migration but it had to stop due to the political pressure. Similarly, the idea of issuing Unique Identity Card to the citizen of India to create a differentiation between the natives and migrants has not taken off fully because of administrative and official constraints. Further increased surveillance and border fences have helped to some extent but not fully because some of the corrupt BSF personnel and vested economic and political interests have reduced the effectiveness of border control. Thus, the Indian government has not fully successful in the preventing the illegal migrations from Bangladesh but analysts have suggested that providing work permits and livelihood opportunities would help to resolve the problems (Das 2016).

The Pakistani state is more critical and strict towards the Afghan migrants especially after Peshwar attacks in 2014 as those who have lived in Pakistan for decades are forced to go back to their home country. The Human Right Watch claims that Pakistani police have pursued an unofficial policy of punitive retribution that has included raids on Afghan settlements, harassments, detention and physical violence. But the Pakistani officials have a different view on it as one of the officials stated that the police is directed under the counter terrorism 'National Action Plan' to scan the habitations of suspected of supporting Taliban and other extremists groups. The United Nations High Commissioner for Refugees (UNHCR) representative Indrika Ratwatte has observed, "if our key programmes in the areas of education and youth empowerment for Afghan refugees do not get adequate resources, young people without options and possibilities either here or in their home country will look for greener pastures" (Dominguez 2015).

The role of state is also very important in preserving the rights of the immigrants. There are a number of provision are existing for the protection of migrants rights globally by United Nations (UN) and International Labour Organization (ILO) which are determined to migrants workers against exploitation, protect their rights to social security and prevent them from discriminatory practices and these human right instruments are apply to everyone irrespective of their national identity. Migrant workers can claim their rights through these legal instruments only if the country has ratified the conventions and protocols of UN and ILO from which they have emigrated. No country of South Asia has ratified the conventions of ILO but the convention of UN has been ratified by Sri Lanka (1996) and signed by Bangladesh (1998) (Srivastava & Pandey 2017). At regional level, South Asian Association for Regional Co-operation (SAARC) and Colombo Process have been engaging themselves in a consultative process for the protection of rights and security of the immigrants. Countries in South Asia have also undertaken a number of policy measures to deal with the recruitment process and cost of migration but they have not been able to make any comprehensive policy steps towards a check on irregular / illegal migration.

Conclusion

South Asian continent is a region of developing countries where economies are not as mature as in the developed countries. Also they have volatile socioeconomic and political background. With the growing number of cities, people are moving from one place to another for better job opportunities which led to huge internal displacement in countries itself. But in the last few decades, people are tending to cross border to achieve better resources of livelihood. These cross border movement are not guided by any regional consensus or policy framework which create chaos in the region and providing loopholes for the people associated with illegal activities or trying to threaten the state.

It is important for countries to initiate bilateral and multilateral agreements over immigration and create a policy framework related to it. Regional associations (such as SAARC) can be effectively use as a platform for this. It is the responsibility of the state to draft a strong policy not only against illegal activities generated by migration but also to protect the rights of migrants and help them to prosper in every possible manner.

References

Dominguez, Gabriel (2015), little Help for 'Mistreated' Afghans in Pakistan, www.*deutschewelle.com*, Germany 18 November 2015.

Srivastava, Ravi & Pandey, Arvind Kumar (2017), *Internal and International Migration in South Asia: Drivers, Interlinkage and Policy Issue*, United Nations Educational Scientific and Cultural Organization (UNESCO), New Delhi.

Das Pushpita (2016), *Illegal Migration from Bangladesh: Deportation, Border Fences and Work Permits*, Institute for Defense Studies & Analyses, New Delhi.

AHN, Pong-Sul (2005), Prospects and Challenges of Out Migration from South Asia and its neighbouring Countries, *Labour & Development, Vol. 11, no. 1, June, 2005.*

Bharadwaj, Vinod K., Migration and Security in South Asia: Emeerging Challeenges and Concerns.

Alimia, Sanaa (2012), Afghans in Pakistan Face a Perilous Future, *www.aljazeera.com, 29 July 2012.*

Kulkarni, Nisha Kumar (2013), Tracking Urban Poverty Trends in India, Bangladesh, Nepal and Pakistan, *Searchlight South Asia, March 2013, Vol. 4, Issue 6.*

Sharma et al. (2015), *Migration in South Asia: A Review*, Population Council, New Delhi.

Human Right Watch (2016), *Pakistan: Renewed Threats to Afghan Refugees (Extended Legal Residency Status through 2017)*, New York.

Abraham, Rhea (2013), The Afghanistan Refugee Crisis: Implication for Pakistan and Iran, *Air Power Journal Vol. 8, No. 3, Monsoon 2013 (July- September)*, New Delhi.

Chapter Nine

Understanding Migration and Human Security: Trends and Implications of Bangladeshi Migrants in India

Oindrila Datta Gupta

Abstract

Security as a dominant theme in IR scholarship has been mainly statist in its theorisation. The paper wishes to problematize the idea of security and examine the non traditional security concerns that loom large today. South Asian security structure involves military-political factors playing a vital role but the non-military security issues have also encompassed the arena of security. The traditional notions of security will be deconstructed and human security as a concept will be explored. The research puzzle is how the cross border migration brings with it a baggage of chronic human security threats such as hunger, fear, diseases, environmental pressure, exploitation etc. which often threatens the state and society. The paper delves into migration issue between India and Bangladesh as a fulcrum of diplomacy and conflict between the two and investigates its impact on India's socio-political-economic stability with rising ethnic conflicts and informalisation of economy especially in the cities.

Introduction

Security has occupied a chief theme in both the mainstream and critical theories in International Relations. The mainstream security theories have emphasised on statist approach focussing on the nation states, military dimensions and regional security frameworks. The theories emphasised on the political and national security examining the strategic relations with the neighbouring countries for ensuring border safety against encroachments, enemy threats, power balances which cannot be overlooked in terms of national interests. Security is therefore important not for the individual survival but also for the preservation of state's sovereignty (Chatterjee 2011). It is crucial to rethink and deconstruct the concept of security in the literature of international relations for understanding the contemporary challenges that confront the states such as the issues of food security, environmental security, energy, health, women security and trafficking in drugs, money laundering, thereby broadening the avenue of the discourse. Moving beyond the conventional contours of security where territoriality and state interests were prime concerns, it is also vital to come out of the rigid polarisation of traditional and non traditional security concerns. International Relations has stepped into constitution of security matrix which provides diverse perspective on analysing varied forms of security threats that were neglected by the dominant theories. As P.R. Chari (in Banerjee 2000:41-58 quoted in Mallavarapu 2008) has observed:

> '...the narrow view of security does not reflect the realities underlying national and regional security within the international system. Issues like the struggle for resources embedded in the pursuit of energy security, food security and more lately, environmental security. Apart from that, the security implications of regional global problems associated with overpopulation, such as, environmental degradation and resource depletion, forced migrations, international terrorism, ascendancy of non-state actors in drugs, arms, money-laundering and financial crime organizations; and the growing linkages between governance and international security, reflect the more complex verities of international security.'

The article seeks to look at the migration as an important security issue which not only threats the national security but also bring challenges to the human security. It is important to understand the South Asian countries deal with the migration as a security threat to the socioeconomic and political stability which is one of the biggest challenges to the region with porous borders. The policy coordination becomes vital to control the unlimited flows of migrants with the help of cooperation from various countries, institutions and legal mechanisms which impacts overall efficiency of managing the migration and ensuring the security of the people. Theoretical analysis of security and the migration issue captures not only the threat of illegal migration on state sovereignty and security but also how the process impacts the migrants mainly women by exposing themselves to several vulnerabilities and exclusion from any state protection. Revolving around the policy instruments, measures, mechanisms and role of civil society in combating human security challenges pertaining to migration, recommendations will be provided to contest migration and security challenges thrown before the state and society.

Conceptualising Human Security

Security has been also conceptualized by Indian scholars explicitly like Rajesh Basrur (2001) in terms of military security (nuclear threat, territorial aggression); economic security (food, clothing, shelter, employment); securing quality life (environmental, political stability) and admits that in case of South Asia state still remains the primary agency for assuring security. Classical realists like Morgenthau (1997) had underlined interests as power in determining the state behavior as the tenets of realist theory of International relations dismissing the non-traditional security threats. The traditional realists had highlighted the distinction between high politics and soft politics, where the former emerging from the state as the key reference point of security. However, even in the words of Morgenthau the normative arena is also available for explaining the conflicts and security notions even though the statism cannot be avoided and also that the soft politics and norms remain a low priority. Waltz (1979) in his structural realism emphasizes on security than power which is the prime concern of the state. Similarly, Stephen Walt (2002) had stressed on the military power for securitization of the states whereby he underlined the shift towards the non-traditional security studies will defy the 'intellectual coherence' of the field and further that '...it would be irresponsible for the security studies community to ignore the central questions that form the heart of the security studies field.' Even while probing into the third world countries the security studies remain realist in its context such as Mohammad Ayoob (1997) in his idea of subaltern realism who explains the nuances of third world states where state is valued as it has the authority as the political and administrative entity for security of the territory. For him, security is characterized as political and used in terms of territory and institution. Security/insecurity is defined in context of external and internal vulnerabilities that weaken the state structures in the system. The other kinds of insecurity or weakness such as environmental, economic, food are part of study only if they are acute enough to threaten the state institutions, its political outcomes that will affect the boundaries of the state, capacity of the government.

In contrast the liberals have emphasized on the human needs, their concern for the development, and peace by dismissing the binaries of high politics and soft politics where the military security does not stand as first priority over environmental, economic security. In this context liberalism provides a space for non-traditional security concerns. The Copenhagen security studies also provide a critique of the dominant security literature and tried to provide an inclusive approach to the security studies. Barry Buzan, Ole Waever (1991) have developed that securitization explains who securitizes, on what issues of threat, for whom (the object of the security) and for what purpose, under what conditions to acquire desired results. They have shown strong interest in regional security dynamics and undertook a relational security concept in International Relations. By problemetising the dominant discourse they emphasise on the social perspective to security fashioning the basic idea of security as a social category emerging from the political practice. Security as a concept has seen varied colours in International Relations explained by scholars from different perspective. While realists remain skeptical of including human security in traditional study of state sovereignty and security parameters, the other quarters of scholars aim to broaden the parameter of security by including the human aspect along with state as a referent object. The debates and discussions pertaining to the content of security have led to the diversity of opinion and analysis calling for sensitivity towards the idea of human security. Ronald Paris had argued that the definition of UNDP on human security comprising economic, health, food, environment, personal, community and political security creates an air of discontent and dilemma over the consensus on core security elements. Human security as a subject of security studies has been conceived as examining the ways to secure people, 'a valid paradigm for identifying, prioritizing and resolving emerging transnational security problems' (Thomas and Tow 2002). As pointed out by Bellamy and Mc Donald (2002) the discourse of human security does not aim to diminish the role of states and does not devalue the importance of sovereignty when it aims at protecting the executor of human wrongs; neither does it challenge the international economic system and the political structure of states. Hence for many international relations scholars it has a limited importance in the security studies. However as the world is confronted with whole range of issues outside the border encroachment challenging the core concepts of national security human security has become an alternative to the realpolitik focusing on balance of power, security dilemma and military doctrines. In South Asia, national security has always figured in top of the hierarchy of interests due to the creation of states as a result of colonial politics for the purpose of securing the state sovereignty and territory. The idea of human security started gaining currency as Asian nation states while emphasizing on state centric national security also focused on the development of the state economically, politically and socially. The idea can be traced back to the inclusive security concept as propounded by W. Blatz's (1966) theory of individual security. Developing from this, the UN Human Development Report 1994 had defined human security as "safety from chronic threats such as hunger, disease, and repression as well as protection from sudden and harmful disruptions in the pattern of daily life." In this report, a chapter entitled "New Dimensions of Human Security" characterised the term as universal, interdependent, preventive and people centric (1994: 22-23) broadening the concept of security by making it inclusive, open-ended with its focus on freedom from want and fear. As Mahbub ulHaq (1995:115) had exclaimed:

> *"...the world is entering a new era in which the very concept of security will change – and change dramatically. Security will be interpreted as: security of people, not just territory, Security of individuals, not just nations, Security through development, not through arm, Security of all the people everywhere – in their homes, in their jobs, in their streets, in their communities, in their environment."*

The human security negating the status-quoism in the traditional theorisation where state was the principle unit of analysis for the survival and the key questions in the human security debate is "security for whom?" postulating the core ideas of human rights and equality, environmental backlash and resource crisis to which national security had been indifferent. In contemporary times, human pandemics like food shortage, environmental damage, ethnic wars, violation of rights, political persecution leads to rise of refugee problem, population pressure (Michael Renner 1996). International Commission on Intervention and State Sovereignty (ICISS 2001), The Responsibility to Protect mentioned that human security today is indispensible and indivisible in the interdependent world. The human security discourse brings a rigorous debate not only between the realists and the liberals where the later concentrates on the human freedom and security in the international system. The focal point of the notion is that human security is as important as the international security (Burgess and Gräns 2012: 101). The nature of conflict has also changed over the period of time as states are not just engaged in the border related conflicts but also on the issue of resources, inability of governance which endangers the life of citizens at national and international level such as violence, military and armed conflict, underdevelopment, diseases, climate change (Human Security Centre 2005).

The final report of Commission on Human Security entitled *Human Security Now,* defines human security as:

> "...to protect the vital core of all human lives in ways that enhance human freedoms and human fulfillment. Human security means protecting fundamental freedoms – freedoms that are the essence of life. It means protecting people from critical (severe) and pervasive (widespread) threats and situations. It means using processes that build on people's strengths and aspirations. It means creating political, social,environmental, economic, military and cultural systems that together give people the building blocks of survival, livelihood and dignity." (CHS: 2003: 4)

Human security as a concept requires a holistic approach that encompasses the use of new opportunities to handle the threats not only in an integrated manner but through interdependent mechanisms involving development, human rights and national security. It emphasizes on the inter linkage between the threats and institutional mechanisms to counter threats such as conflicts and war that leads to poverty and deprivation which culminates into the health insecurities like infectious diseases, malnutrition. It can also pave way towards political insecurities such as instability, corruption, human rights violation; inter community conflicts which further leads to international disruptions. It is important to understand that there is a relation between development and conflict and the role of state and non state actors in addressing the human security is as vital as addressing the national security, conflicts. Several institutions mainly United Nations, African Union have several programmes which specifically addresses the challenges to human security. "Human Security complements state security, strengthens human development and enhances human rights" (Commission on Human Security 2003: 2). It acknowledges that non-traditional insecurities generates tensions in the society and therefore the concept of human security and state security are interdependent as without the former later is also not attainable. Today the idea of human security is well acceptable as a doctrine of foreign policy and an international strategy for development as well as a tool for institutionalizing the processes of humanitarianism. It aims to focus on the good governance, social protection, and democratic policies by undertaking a bottom up approach to make it more people centric. Thereby the concept is multi-sectoral, multi-dimensional cutting across different states, communities and it includes a complex interdependence and interaction between local, national, regional, international levels capturing various contexts within which insecurities and threats are felt (United Nations 2009).

Contextualising Migration as a Human Security Issue

Migration today has become a strategic precedence as the security steps out of the traditional military concepts to human risks that's involves the inclusion of multilateral institutions and several security frameworks. The security patterns for combating migration are to encompass the global and intra regional policies along with the national policies to strengthen the state institutions. The human mobility across borders brings with it not only a threat to border security but also risks of economic, environmental, demographic insecurity as Keohane et al (1999:2) remarked "genuine security requires not only the absence of or protection against a military threat, but also the management of a multitude of risks concerning the political economic, and social well-being of states and their peoples". Previously migration was taken as a tool for bargaining the economic relations between the states where migrants were not seen as the threat to the nation sovereignty, however, with the inflow of illegal migrants had brought the possible dangers which required state and inter regional cooperation.

Migration, as a concept, is defined by International Organisation for Migration as "the movement of people across the international border or within their respective state." It includes the migration of persons as refugees, displaced people, and economic migrants along with the family or fleeing from the political persecution, famine, natural disaster. United Nations reports have observed that as the numbers of migrants are increasing it is to be understood as a phenomenon of complex and interconnected flows of people, services, money and goods. With globalization the flow of commodities, money have been encouraged but the protectionist policies of the western government in the recent times acts as a stumbling block to the movement of humans with range of new regulations and migrant policies. The states are using the migration control measures to showcase their sovereign power over their territory as they become the determining factor of who may enter and reside in their respective land and thus frame the legal provisions to for managing the border and movement in consensus with the international law and human rights. With the rise of undocumented, illegal and irregular migrants the governments are becoming more vigilant as these migrants operate outside the regulatory frameworks without any travel documents or valid passport and they do not even fulfill any administrative obligations.

The nexus between migration and security focuses on the aspects pertaining to the national security as the undocumented, hidden and illegal migration can lead to unlawful activities such as terrorism, drug, human trafficking. As Khalid Koser (2011) argues, 'the perception of migration as a threat to national security has certainly heightened in recent years, in part in response to the rapid rise in the number of international migrants (...) and especially of 'irregular' or 'illegal' migrants.' The focus on the interconnection between the two migrations and security has embraced the concept of human security as it challenges not only the state sovereignty but also placed the migrants as an object and subject of threats. 'The structural violence that causes many to migrate, the impact of deportation and detention policies and the hazards to personal safety of migrants resulting from the increasing reluctance of states to offer sanctuary to those genuinely in need are just some of the aspects of the nexus between migration and human security.' When migration is taken as a national security issue culminating into the stringent rules of surveillance, deportation has led to human security concerns for the migrants which encourage them to undertake hazardous ways to survive in the host countries often getting trapped in the networks of smuggling, trafficking. However the human security challenges to the migrants are often shadowed by the national security concerns. Kerwin has remarked that 'human security is often set against the concept of national security, but the two need not be at odds. Properly crafted national security policies should further human security. However, the human security framework moves the migration discussion beyond national security's narrow preoccupation with border control, detention, and the criminalization of migrants, and opens it to the conditions of insecurity that drive irregular and crisis migration. Human security also asks whether policies developed out of a misguided view of national security put people in less secure positions, like the hands of traffickers and smugglers.'

It can be argued that managing the issue of migration as national security and human security agenda is a complex task of balancing and poses a challenging task especially to the less developed countries mainly in the global south where these countries are destination, transit points of migrants. Migration today is not simply a north-south phenomenon but also south-south. In the developing countries of global south the indifference to the rights such as human rights, labour rights of the migrants especially the illegal migrants that draws more uncertainty as they get plugged in the informal markets which has no social security. Securitization of migrants becomes a global issue as the modern telecommunication revolution and transportation motivates the people to travel and settle for better life. The Human Development Report invites the humane approach to the migration study and the integration of migrants with the residents makes the society wider, diverse and culturally complementary.

Bangladeshi Migrants and Issue of Human Security: Contestations and Negotiations

In India the influx of migrants from neighbouring countries like Bangladesh, Nepal has raised serious apprehensions about the border securities and social imbalances that grow with the entry of people. The growth of radicalism, fundamentalism, demographic changes and intrusion of nation's "sovereign space" (Behera 2011) have negative consequences on the political-economic environment. As the South-South migration takes place due to contiguous borders, it has positive impacts in terms of cheap labour and on other hand it has negative externalities in terms of economic, cultural clashes as well as carrier of health issues such as AIDs, tuberculosis, infections which spread mainly due to incapacity of the state to manage the undocumented migration.

As per the United Nations Department of Economic and Social Affairs (2009) India had accounted for almost 2.5 percent of the international migrants in 2010 as India shares international borders inviting migrants mainly from Bangladesh, Nepal and Tibet due to cultural and historical affinities with India. The geographical contiguity, socio-cultural and linguistic similarities make the borders vulnerable to migration. India has the longest border with Bangladesh along the states of West Bengal, Assam, Tripura, and Meghalaya and in the border fencing only 1500 km has barbed fencing whereas the majority of borders mainly those which are riverine are porous to the migrants. The illegal migrants in the north eastern states and West Bengal are often difficult to measure and locate mainly because they integrate with the native population very easily making the migration control more complex creating pressure on the resources such as land, water, employment and services.

Most of the migrants from Bangladesh are relatively poorer coming from the rural areas belonging to the vulnerable and poverty stricken sections of the society with lower levels of education, unskilled migrate to the nearby urban regions of Indian state moving towards the informalisation of urban employment sector. There are approximately 3 million of Bangladeshi migrant workers presently in India who are engaged in informal sector such as domestic work, construction industry, labour force in daily work basis, rag pickers, rickshaw pullers who enter the bordering states due to political instability, economic distress, environmental backlash such as floods, storms, cyclones which displaces the poor from their livelihood. The undocumented migrants from Bangladesh are pushed into the Indian states with the help of brokers and middle men who play a vital role in cross border human movement. There are also instances of engaging border officials in the migration process, moreover much of the Indo-Bangladesh border corridors are not well guarded due to discrepancy in the demarcation especially those across the water bodies. There are also hardly any female border officials who can keep a check on the migrants and thus the female migration creates a circuit of sex trafficking. Many of the female workers are also plugged in the bonded labour susceptible to the exploitation; abuse which often goes unreported (Bashir Uddin 2014).

Environmental crisis in Bangladesh and the impact of global warming, climate change have been crucial factors for cross-border migration. The coastal migration in the island of Sundarbans in search of livelihood also suffer from landlessness, unemployment, disparities of income distribution, violation of human rights, inaccessibility to the basic amenities since the undocumented migrants donot have the address proof or any identity card to access the resources. It has been estimated that since 2010 the migrants from Bangladesh constituted the largest flow of migrants who resided in India and as per the World Bank estimates there are around 3.3 million migrants across from Bangladesh-India corridor (2011:6) due to the historic links between the two countries. The influxes of migrants have contributed in the labour pool of skilled and unskilled workers where the latter comprises quite a large number of illegal and seasonal migrants across borders. The bordering cities, villages have many cross border trade linkages in form of cotton industries, agriculture and other economic prospects which continue to be a source of income, informal remittances to their home country. The Bangladeshi migrants who cross the borders paying the agents and brokers for quick channels to move through the migration corridor are unable to acquire the legal permit which are required to work in India and they often operate as regular day to day migrants who come to the neighbouring states in the daytime and go back to the home country after daily work. The economic reasons behind employing the illegal migration is also the rationale of paying them low wages, their willingness to work for longer hours at lower rates due to the economic distress back home. Moreover, the lack of organisational support and knowledge about their labour rights they are often trapped in the web of labour exploitation which are some of the main factors that enable the migration process to sustain which invites crisis in the security conditions of the migrants especially girls, women who are often forced into prostitution, child labour as they are the most vulnerable while they cross the river islands, treacherous valleys and hills (Hazarika 2000). The economic pressures, rapid growth of population, land unavailability, economic insecurity, starvation, and natural disasters have been major steering factor in the Bangladeshi influx (Samaddar 1999). As the new trend of migration moves towards feminisation the migration corridor today can see entry of women in the labour market especially in the urban labour pool which changes their roles and status in the society. However, it is not say that these women who cross the borders donot face any gender related hurdles as they have to face impoverishment as they don't have equal access to formal routes of migration, information, legalities. Their migration is marred with insecurities as there are no safety nets or social security provisions becoming the victim of flesh trade and human trafficking network in pretext of jobs. Moreover, it has been evident that women migrants face the threats of rape, sexual assault, exploitation by the border guards, agents thereby forcing the women to enter the sex trade. The flow of people between the states and across the region results in human security problems mainly in the events o armed conflict, war as in case of Bangladesh Liberation war in 1971 which led to a large number of refugees to India who had no security legislation and migration regulation to protect the refugees from any atrocities which they face.

Bangladesh also faces the brunt of environmental insecurity where people's lives are miserably affected by the intensified natural disaster. The rising level of sea, disappearing islands, increasing pressure over which also leads to environmental conflict. The United Nation Inter Governmental Panel on Climate Change (IPCC) has predicted that there is likelihood that Bangladesh may lose nearly one fifth of its land by 2050 due to rising sea levels as a result of global warming. In 2014, Bangladesh has been ranked 1st on the Climate Change Vulnerability.

Index and fifth in the Global Climate Risk Index 2015 (Kreft et al., 2015) and as per the IDMC (2015) report on South Asia which considers Bangladesh as one of the most-at-risk countries, facing the danger of future climate change impacts causing environmental degradation manifested all over the country. The most vulnerable part is the southern portion of Bangladesh that is subjected to cyclones, storm surge, salinity intrusion, coastal line erosion, water logging, and potential sea-level rising causing a deadly situation for the people.

No strict measures are specified to ensure environmental security even though committees and authorities to look into disasters caused by natural force are appointed such as BCCSAP in 2009 and NAPA 2005. The floods in 2005 in districts of Bangladesh had forced half a million people to migrate from their home and clusters of people have to find shelter in the urban slums of India. In 2009, the cyclone Aila had killed 190 people with 4.82 million people affected in the nearby coastal region (Leighton et al. 2011 in IOM report). The environmental threats have coaxed the inhabitants of Bangladesh to cross the borders to save life is giving birth to the environmental refugees which has become a serious issue between the two nations as the influx also leads to population pressure in the north eastern states and West Bengal which also has political implications leading to ethnic conflicts, riots. The impact of climate change on the small island, coastal states also constitutes political, economic, societal threats to the community thereby becoming a national survival issue. As people migrate without any adaptation measures they are vulnerable to vector borne diseases often causing death as they lack suitable access to health care services. The inhabitants in the enclave areas and coastline are the worst hit as they face not only the wrath of nature but also problems related to sanitation and water borne diseases such as diarrhea, dysentery, fever, cholera, typhoid; vector borne diseases such as malaria, dengue which kills thousands due to lack of health care services. Due to floods many people face shortages of food and loss of jobs as the lands get submerged causing damage of crops, infrastructure. Cyclones affecting all the sectors in places like Khulna, Sunamganj, Patuakhali followed by storm surge have the most devastating impact on the educational and health sectors since the natural disasters lead to damage of educational resources like books, schools are shifted to new areas leading to the disruption of the education and the livelihoods of the people become uncertain and temporary. The hazardous climate induced changes have led to the damage of agricultural land which deprives them of the employment and erratic rainfall in some areas as well as drought in few areas like Rajshahi leads to food crisis in several parts of the country. Moreover, the rise of arsenic contamination, river erosion, receding groundwater, earthquakes has become key factors in migration across the region.

In India, there is a growing concern about undocumented and illegal migration from Bangladesh which has its social and political consequences in Indian villages and urban landscape. Frequent instances of riots between locals and migrants which are often violent in character are becoming a daily affair in the north eastern states of India, West Bengal (Shamshad 2013). It has been reiterated by several scholars and in the media that there is no official estimate of the total number of undocumented Bangladeshi migrants in India.Thapliyal (2000) also considers that flows of migrants have become a major concern for the politics, fight for vote banks and highlights the alteration in the socio-economic structure of the bordering states due to the immigration of Bangladeshi workers. Partho Ghosh (2009) considers illegal immigration as a political issue as Bangladeshi immigrants have an impact on the vote bank while destabilizing the demographics. Each country has labour laws covering a range of issues, from freedom of collective bargaining and formation of unions to provision of social security benefits (including maternity protection, occupational safety and health) to labourers working in different sectors, but other than in India there is no specific law focusing exclusively on migrant labour.

Countries	1990	2000	2010	2016
Afghanistan	3.43	2.52	3.09	3.33
Bangladesh	1.07	1.55	3.42	3.98
Bhutan	0.0004	0.0007	0.005	0.009
India	3.36	5.15	10.70	13.02
Nepal	0.22	0.29	0.78	1.06
Pakistan	1.40	2.01	3.82	4.48
Sri Lanka	0.60	0.78	1.27	1.47
Maldives	0.0003	0.0006	0.0011	0.0013
South Asia	10.08	12.31	23.08	27.22

Source: Calculated from International Migration Stock-2015, UN DESA

The migrants not only face political discrimination but also in terms of getting wages, proper work quality and conditions under which they are employed; less access to the food security, social security, beneficiary cards are not provided to them (Srivastava and Sasikumar 2003). Migrants also face socio-cultural and linguistic discrimination, poor housing conditions, mob violence which also have consequences on them mentally leading to loneliness, depression often making them engaged in crime related activities. The environmental degradation and depletion of resources lead to movement of human across borders and lead to the conflict over the distribution of resources and income.

The Global south today because of the increasing undocumented migrants have become the focus of academic attention. It therefore becomes essential to adopt measures to secure the migrants against the exploitation, adoption of measures to protect the migrants against exploitation. The government policies have looked into various issues related to safety and security of the migrants in the urban centres. As most of the migrants settle in the slums they are deprived of resources as the identities of these people remain blurred because they do not get registered to acquire the services of the government. As the Calcutta Research Group on migration observe, Kolkata has been the city of migrants that have experienced a large influx of migrants in terms of refugees during the post partition period in 1950s and later with the creation of Bangladesh which created the pressure on the state government to provide them with rehabilitation packages to settle in camps, provide training to the men and women for finding a suitable job while the state government had to repeatedly resolve the issues of housing, slum management, population density, outbreak of diseases and scarcity of land. The government thereby looked outwards in the making of new township which could accommodate the excess population and the new housing schemes are implemented to provide shelter to the growing number and prevent the rising informal settlements with no access to safe drinking water, sanitation as the task of improving the urban landscape under the Kolkata Municipal Corporation. The government not only had to manage the urban infrastructural issues but also the matters pertaining to social justice and segregation between the insiders and outsiders which often culminated in violent clashes. The role of civil societies in form of different organization delved into the problems arising from the relation between migration and urbanization. As the migrants clustered in the city it also raised the price of the real estate and transformed the work-labour relations. The coexistence of neoliberalism and urbanization also postulated the growth of capitalist accumulation which brought about changes in employment structure, social fabric including the formation of new identities, mixed identities which give the city and neighbouring areas a new colour. While there are many women migrants who are engaged in the tasks such as rag pickers, waste picking which expose them to the struggle for home, food and are often subjected to abuse and exploitation. Some of the women who migrate try to get themselves registered as 'ayah' or care givers at home. However, now they demand passport size photos and identity cards which make getting employment difficult.

Moreover, as urbanization expands rapidly and the rise of mega cities the demand for domestic workers, care givers, servants, security guards increase, the cities become a magnet to attract more migrants and sadly India does not have any registration system as in China which prevented squatter settlements. In case of north eastern cities and Kolkata they become transit points for the Bangladeshi migrants to enter into rest of India, mainly flocking into big cities such as Delhi, Mumbai where they are engaged in the semi-skilled, unskilled, casual workers by residing in the slums are also subjected to the threat to the clearance of the slums by the municipalities who want to project their cities as global cities/world cities. Similarly, in Mumbai which suffers from high housing prices giving rise to the largest slum in the region, the state government with the help of NGOs makes an attempt to secure the rights of those who are displaced for making the city clean and globally appealing. The slum dwellers comprising mainly the migrants suffer from the uncertainty of survival as many of them do not have any identity proofs, certificate to dwell legally and become victims of air borne and water borne diseases. As the cities get more dominated by the elites and waves of globalization, the slum dwellers and the undocumented migrants settled suffer from eviction since they are not citizens and cannot acquire the services of state such as Housing for All, social welfare, health care, that will limit the access to the urban spaces. Most of the slum areas and the illegal occupants are labeled as encroachers, the Maharashtra Slum Areas Act for example introduced the idea of cut off date and anybody residing at a particular place before the date will not be evicted and will also be given compensation. As the image of cities is fast changing as the urban poor are taken as burden and their stay in the urban spaces are criminalized often violating their human rights to stay in a dignified manner. The NGOs, human rights activists have protested against the deportation of illegal migrants like in case of Muslim Bengali speaking migrants who illegally settled in Mumbai were deported back to Kolkata; however the initiative halted due to the protests from West Bengal. The anti-migrant policies by the political parties and the state police have threatened and abused the illegal migrants, where the anti migrant environment have created socio-political and economic confusion as migrant workers are essential to the manufacturing industries. Often the ghettoisation of the migrant workers has also led to the formation of migrant working class solidarity in the cities for securitizing themselves against discrimination or violation of rights.

The discourse on migration also shows that the vulnerable sections like women and children who are frequently trapped into the web of prostitution, sex trade, trafficking especially to Middle East while migrating from Bangladesh to India live in the world of informal job market with no social security against exploitation but the growing protective laws against the illegal activities also aim to give security to the illegal migrants. It is important for the Bangladesh government to keep records of the women and men migrating outside and for the purpose of their migration. However, due to the official restrictions imposed on the women, they often take the help of private agents to help them which informalises the route of movements. In the contemporary times there are many global forums on women migration especially in the south-south migration corridor to analyse the issues and problems of the networks through which the mobility takes place. The border management becomes important to curtail the problem of illegal migration not only to prevent any threat to the security of the nation but also to ensure that the illegal route does not make the migrants succumb to risky adventures as they cross the borders. The Border Security Force has tried very often to deport the illegal migrants however the Bangladesh government has maintained that these are all Indian citizens and not Bangladeshi migrants. Scholars like Chirantan Kumar (2009) has reported that the rigid oppressive policies of the government against the minorities, lack of job opportunities have forced them to migrate into India. The securitization of the borders will help in curbing the risks of smuggling, drug peddling, illegal arms transfer, theft, crimes against women, terrorist activities; however given the linguistic and ethnic affinities we share with the bordering nation efforts are needed from sides to curb illegal movements and not to make borders a point of harassment for the people to cross borders. The migrant workers may be utilized for unskilled and semi skilled provides proper legislations are framed where the migrants are protected of their human rights and do not become a burden to the receiving nation. There are existent laws like Migrant Workmen act 1979 but not many efforts have been made to make it functional, moreover Bangladesh has also not ratified the 1990 UN Convention on the Protection of the Rights of All Migrant Workers and Members of their Families even though Bangladesh is a signatory. The main reason behind not ratifying the convention is that the receiving nation may be unwilling to recruit any Bangladeshi labourers for work (Kibria 2011). Hence, the need of the hour is that the government, policy makers, academicians and the scholars need to find solutions to the issue of migration and ensure the human security so that they are not subjected to inhuman conditions and treatments to address the South-South migration in a sensible manner rather than simply politicizing it.

Conclusion

The increasing migration in the South-South corridor shows that the family ties, ethnic and linguistic similarities, wage differences and the geographical proximity play vital role.

Process of border making has political underpinnings to it. The borderlands of South Asia are colonial handiwork. Sir Cyrill Radcliffe had confessed that he was unable to draw a contiguous boundary between the eastern part of India and East Pakistan (Banerjee 2010). Borders are also social construct.. Inclusion and exclusion takes place in this process. Migration often leads to a creation of new geopolitical space and the self-others identity looms large. Borders are complex because it reflects the political, social and economic currents. With new kinds of threats arising with growing number of terrorist activities borders are a zone of securitization taken by the state(Newman2006). Indo–Bangladesh migration shows the historical factors that have made the flow of human continuous and complex. The patterns have however changed over the period of time with economic globalisation. Where migration as a topic always gets politicized it is difficult to say how far the problem will be resolved. It also requires a centre – state cooperation. The process of pushing the Bangladeshis to their home and Bangladesh refusing to accept seems to be regular affair. There is also a connection to migration and global economy since the trend of migration shows that the inflow is from the under developed poverty stricken country, hence, it is important that the financial support to uplift the economic status is provided to Bangladesh which can create more jobs and sources of livelihood. This will prevent the intensity and frequency of migration to the neighbouring states of Indo-Bangladesh border and will reduce the burden on Indian economy and security matrix. Security cooperation is the most essential requirement in the South Asian scenario whereby the focus is not necessarily on the militarization of the borders but also the security of human beings whether residents or migrants to live with human dignity. Cooperation from the Bangladeshi government is necessary to curb the problem of illegal migrants who not only cause social strife and religious riots but also integrate with many separatists groups. India should carve out its own migration policies which will restrict the movement of illegal migrants with the help of brokers, thereby the government can secure the nation of unauthorized activities such as smuggling, terrorism as well as the securitize of people by protecting their rights and liberties. It also becomes the responsibility of the nation to balance between the national security and human security.

References

Acharya, A. (1997) 'The Periphery as the Core: The Third World and Security Studies' in Keith Krause and Michael C. Williams ed. *Critical Security Studies: Concepts and Cases* (London: UCL Press, pp.299-327.

Ayoob, M. (1997) 'Defining Security: A Subaltern Realist Perspective', in Keith Krause and Michael C. Williams, ed. *Critical Security Studies: Concepts and Cases,* London: UCL Press, 1997, pp.121-146.

Bajpai, K. (2003) 'The Idea of Human Security', *International Studies*, Vol.40, No.3, 2003, pp.195-228.

Bellamy, A and Mc Donald, M.(2002) The Utility of Human Security': Which Humans? What Security? A Reply to Thomas & Tow, *Security Dialogue*, vol 33 issue 2, p 373-377.

Behera, S. (2011) *Trans-Border Identities: A Study on the Impact of Bangladeshi and Nepali Migration to India.* Policy Series No. 1. ICRIER, New Delhi.

Bashir, U. (2014), Human trafficking in South Asia: Issues of Corruption and Human Security *International Journal of Social Work and Human Services Practice*

Banerjee, P, Hazarika, S., Hussain, M., & Samaddar, R. (1999) *Indo-Bangladesh Cross-Border Migration and Trade.* EPW, 34(36), 2549.

Buzan, B.(1991) *People, State and Fear: An Agenda for International Security Studies in the Post Cold War Era*, Boulder, Colorado: Lynne Reinner Publishers.

Buzan B and O. Waever, (2003)*Regions and Powers. The Structure of International Security,* Cambridge University Press, Cambridge.

Burgess, P. and Gräns, J. (2012) 'Human Security', in Snyder, C. A. (ed.) *Contemporary security and strategy.* Third edition. Basingstoke: Palgrave Macmillan, pp. 89–105.

Basrur, M.R. (2001) ed. *Security in the New Millennium: Views from South Asia*, New Delhi: India Research Press.

Blatz, W. (1966) *Human Security: Some Reflections.* (1966). Toronto: University of Toronto Press.

'Cities, Rural Migrants and the Urban Poor', *Mahanirban Calcutta Research Group, Research Briefs* (ed) available at http://www.mcrg.ac.in, p 1-95, accessed on 29 June 2017.

Chari, P.R. (2000), 'Security Studies in India: Recent Trends and Future Directions' in Banarjee ed. *Security Studies in South Asia: Change and Challenges*, New Delhi: Manohar. pp.41-58

Chatterjee, S. (2011): 'Deconstruction and Double Reading of the South Asian Security Order', in E. Sridharan (ed.), *International Relations Theory and South As*ia, Vol. II , New Delhi: Oxford University Press.

*Commission on Human Security was established in January 2001 in Human Security in Theory and Practicean Overview of the Human Security Concept and the United Nations Trust Fund for Human Security Human Security Unit: United Nations.

Ghosh, Partha S. (2001) *Migrants and Refugees in South Asia: Political and Security Dimension*. Shillong: North Eastern Hill University, pp. 9.

Ghosh, Partha S. (2009) Politics of Competing Ethnicity and Violence: The Experience of India'sNorth East," in *Political Governance and Minority Rights: The South and South-East Asian Scenario*. Lipi Ghosh, ed. (New Delhi, Routledge), pp. 3-30.

*Human Security Centre (2005) *Human Security Report 2005: War and Peace in the 21st Century*. New York. Available at: http://www.hsrgroup.org/human-security-reports/2005/text.aspx, accessed on 25 June 2017.

**Human Security Now,* Human Security Commission(2003), New York: United Nations.

Hazarika, S. (2000) *Rites of Passage: Border Crossings, Imagined Homelands, India's East and Bangladesh*, New Delhi: Penguin Books.

Haq, M. (1995), *Reflections on Human Development*, New York: Oxford University Press, p 115.

*IOM (2001) *In Search of Dreams: Study on the Situation of the Trafficked Women and Children from Bangladesh and Nepal to India*. Geneva: International Organization for Migration, available at http://www.migrationinformation.org/Profiles/display.cfm?ID=848accessed on 30June 2017.

Kibria, N. (2011), "Working Hard for the Money: Bangladesh Faces Challenges of Large-Scale Labor Migration," Migration Information Source, Country Profiles.

Kumar, C. (2009) 'Migration and Refugee Issue between India and Bangladesh', *Scholar's Voice: A New Thinking* 1(1): 64 – 82.

Koser, K.(2011), "When is Migration a Security Issue?' *Brookings,* 31.3. http://www.brookings.edu/research/opinions/2011/03/31-libya-migration-koser accessed on 24 May 2017.

Keohane, R. Aftendorn, H., and C. A. Wallander, (1999) eds., *Imperfect Unions,* Oxford University Press.

Kerwin, D., Human Security, "Civil Society and Migration," *Center for Migration Studies of New York.* Available athttps://docs.unocha.org/sites/dms/HSU/Kerwin%20 statement.pdf accessed on 28 May 2017.

Mallavarpu, S. (2008), *International Relations Theory and Non-Traditional Approaches to Security*, New Delhi: WISCOM

Morgenthau, H. (1997) *Politics Among Nations: A Struggle for Power and Peace,* 6th Edition, Reprint, New Delhi: Kalyani Publishers, p.3.

Narendram, V and Joseph, J. (2013), "Neither Here nor There: An Overview of South-South Migration from both sides of the Bangladesh-India Migration Corridor, *A study commissioned by the International Institute of Social Studies, The Hague (Erasmus University Rotterdam), within the project on 'Migration, Gender and Social Justice', funded by the International Development Research Centre (Canada)* p1-39.

Paris, R. (2001) 'Human Security: Paradigm Shift or Hot Air?', *International Security*, 26(2), pp. 87–102. Available at: http://www.jstor.org/stable/3092123, Accessed: 2 January 2017.

*Population Growth, Demographic Profile of West Bengal and Bangladesh and Illegal Immigration from Bangladesh to India, Part 1, Classified BSF document procured from a BSF source on 29 June 2005, pg. 7

Renner, M. (1996), *Fighting for Survival: Environmental Decline, social Conflict and the new age of Insecurity*, New York and London: W. W. Norton.

Sen, A.(2003) 'Development as Capability Extension' in The Human Development Paradigm' in Fukuda Parr and Shiva Kumar ed. *Readings in Human Development*, New Delhi: Oxford University Press, pp.3-16.

Sammadar, R. (1999) *The Marginal Nation: Trans-Border Migration from Bangladesh To West Bengal.* New Delhi: Sage Publications.

Shamshad, R. (2013) *Politics and Origin of the India-Bangladesh Border Fence,* paper presented at the 17th Biennial Conference of the Asian Studies Association of Australia in Melbourne 1-3

July 2008. Available at :http://artsonline.monash.edu.au/mai/files/2012/07/ rizwanashamshad.pdfaccessed on 17May 2017.

Stephen M. Walt (1991), 'The Renaissance of Security Studies', *International Studies Quarterly*, 35, pp.211-239.

Thapliyal, S. (2000) Bangladeshi Migrants in India: A Cause of Concern. *South Asian Studies*, 35(2).

Thomas, N and Tow, W. (2002) The Utility of Human Security: Sovereignty and Humanitarian Intervention, *Security Dialogue*, Vol 33 issue2,pp. 177-192.

The Right to Protect(2001), Report of The International Commission On Intervention And State Sovereignty, International Commission On Intervention And State Sovereignty, http://responsibilitytoprotect.org/ICISS%20Report.pdf. Accessed on 16July 2017.

UNDP(2000). *Human Development Report*, United Nations Development Programme. New York

United Nations Development Programme (1994) *Human Development Report 1994*. Oxford: Oxford University Press for the UNDP.

Walt,M.S.(2002) 'The Enduring Relevance of the Realist Tradition', in Ira Katznelson & Helen V.Milner, ed. *Political Science: State of the Discipline*, New York & London: W. W. Norton & Company, pp.197-230.

Waltz, K. (1979) *Theory of International Politics*, Massachusetts: Addison-Wesley; 1983; Reprint edition.

Chapter Ten

Migration and Human Security: Meaning, Triggers and Consequences

Aditi Paul

Abstract

The paper examines the concept of migrations as an international phenomenon that has made movement of people a global issue. Migrations is no more a concern of a single or group of states and it is needed to understand this reality and how it is affecting states and its people. Both as a regional and global process, migrations raise pertinent questions about sovereignty, security, identity, means of livelihood, development and private property. Migrations take place for a reason and there are several triggers that not only lead to movement of people but also have an influence on the types of people that migrate. Thereby, migration as a problem is complex. The relationship that migrant people develop with the demography of the host state is most critical in the framing of the policies regarding migrants and their rights and freedom. While harmonization and respect for freedom of human beings is crucial, one must take note that it does affect decisions on citizenship, stateless person, displaced people and so on. There is still much to be done and the responses from states and international organizations are weak and hesitant because migrations challenge the internal and external security paradigms of a sovereign state. Yet, in the era of multiculturalism and globalization of economic chains, it is hard to not accept transnational movement of people and provide them with rights. With so many varied issues linked to migrations, the paper therefore, aims to expand the existing knowledge on migrations and highlight the key issues as well as assess its trends.

Introduction

Before one begins to analyze the problems of migrations and how it is affecting human security, it is preeminent to examine the concept of migrations, not just in a state or region, but as an international phenomenon. It is important to explore questions pertaining to migrations and its dimensions, gender quotient, the push and pull factors, rights of migrant people, and their legal status. Thus, this chapter is a brief examination of international migrations which will equip the reader with concepts to understand the case studies.

Migrations and Its Categories

Migration spread to all parts of the world by the 21st century. Every region witnessed the movement of people and made migration an international phenomenon. Etienne Balibar argues against the restrictive policies and legislations that prevent liberty of movement and selectively allows individuals to circulate (Balibar 2002, 2004).

Migrants are of several types. Some are "worker migrants" who enter a state for a short duration of time and leave. Some migrants are "students" and become part of world mobilizations. Others fall into the category of "family reunification" in which family members of the migrants come and settle with them after the migrant has acquired a legal status in the new state. States like France and United States of America have it in their constitution and immigration policy to grant the right to live with family. On the other hand, some migrants are called "refugees."

While, the categories of migrants are many, the method to segregate and account for the types and permitting them residence and other rights, is a challenge world over. Sometimes, a person falls in the category of migrant, refugee and student at the same time. Sometimes, when babies are born from migrants it becomes difficult to categorize who are nationals and non-nationals. It is an irony that when the border control policies are made stringent, migrants are unable to leave and settle with undefined legal status. And when the borders open, it invites more people as migrants. The transnational nature of migrations has further blurred the distinction between those who came to stay and work for a particular duration, those who are permanent migrants, those who are semi-permanent with residence permit, and those with dual-citizenship.

Regions and Migrations

Migrations take place unevenly. It based on demand and supply. As opposed to the widely held view, people do not necessarily migrate to far off places and rather migrate within the same region. In Latin America, people migrate to Brazil, Argentina, Chile and Venezuela from states like Ecuador, Bolivia, Peru and Colombia. In Europe, the western states like Greece, Germany and Italy witness an influx of migrants from Albania, Poland, Romania and Ukraine. Ireland and United Kingdom purposely opened their border in 2004 to attract migrants as labor from the new members of European Union (EU). However, such forms of migrations have created massive divides within the region in terms of wealth, demographics, ethnicity, religion, etc. For example, the borders between Russia and China or Mexico and USA are home to undocumented border crossings and contrasting mix of people and resources.

The Triggers of Migrations

Evidence has shown that while migrations have taken place both towards South and North of the globe, migrations have been more towards South because the states are developing in nature and attract human resource. Moreover, one cannot overlook the fact that the state borders in the South are porous and lacks stringent border controls as compared to the North.

The economic, social and political disparity in human development accounts for most migrations to occur. When the disadvantaged people gather the knowledge of places through television, internet, mobile phones, networks created by previous migrants, religious associations, etc. that can nourish their dreams of a secure livelihood they exit their home without any consent from the state of origin and enter a new state despite the government's fight against immigration and social unrest. Millions have fled their states due to the political crisis, civil wars and lack of employment. People from Afghanistan, Iraq, Africa, Haiti, Sri Lanka, Bhutan, Nepal, etc. escaped to states of America and Western Europe.

The reasons for migration of whole community, men, women or women with minors to take place are many and varied. Internal push factors within a state, such as religious and ethnic conflicts, lack of job market, search for natural resources like water, oil and minerals, political crisis, rapid urban development, make people migrate. Global warming and environmental questions like desertification, natural disasters, soil depletion, melting of ice, volcanoes, earthquakes, cyclones, etc. displace scores from people each year from their hometown and give rise to concepts like "collective migrants" and "environmentally-displaced persons". For instance, South Asian states like Maldives, Bangladesh and Nepal are perennially under the environmental threats like droughts, cyclones, floods and heavy precipitation. Many living on the shores of the Maldives and Tuvalu Island have fled because of their land beginning to immerse into the sea, salinization, flash floods, rainfall and soil erosion.

Bangladesh has a long history of struggling with an adverse environment that brings in threats like floods and drought. Bangladesh faces the problem of floods in the Himalayan water each year and displaces the poor people. Since India is the closest neighbour and migrants do prefer to enter India often, relations between India and Bangladesh is strained over India providing refuge to the illegal migrants. However, not many are able to migrate and only the poorest fail to seek refuge due to lack of opportunity, knowledge and means to cross the borders.

Nepal witnesses environmentally displaced migrations due to excessive rainfall, landslides and earthquakes. Climate change has led intra-state migrations in Nepal. For instance, during landslides, the people shift to Tarai region. And, during drought, people go back to the lower lands to fetch water. Lying at the northern part of India, Nepalese tend to move to India in search of job, especially during harvest (Sharma and Thapa 2013). Since India has an open border agreement with Nepal, Nepalese do not require documents like work permit and therefore, due to environmental compulsions and search for means of livelihood, they migrate to India. However, "forced migration" is also a trend found common between India and Nepal. Human trafficking from Nepal to other states as a construction laborer, sex worker, beggars, etc. is rampant.

Another trigger of migrations is the search for job. Migrants are people, who are a source of human labor and capital. They are required in abundance in areas like agriculture and construction business. Therefore, sometimes states are dependent upon migrants and plan to invite them. These are called "pull factors" of migrations. For instance, the United Nations Population Division report titled "Replacement Migration" (2001) points out that states of EU, Japan and Russia have ageing population and depend upon migrants for population growth. After the two World Wars, France faced the issue of declining population and for strong economic growth, France had to amass manpower. So, a lot of effort was put into turning non-nationals into French nationals. Foreigners were selectively chosen for encouraging economic boom in France. So, people from Italy, Spain Algeria, Tunisia, Morocco, Turkey and Portugal came and even after entering France illegally, they were registered afterwards.

Interestingly, another reason to invite migrants has been the ageing population in some of the European states. The demand for caregivers from Romania, Poland, Philippines and Ukraine is high. While they are mostly women, such migrants are called "migrant care workers". Thus, one can argue that while EU has strict policies to maintain border checks and refugees, their policies also aims to attract talents and skills for the workforce.

Migrations and the Challenges for the State

An important category of migrants is "forced migrant" or "refugee." Refugee is a related term and the Geneva Convention define sit as "a person who owing to a well-founded fear of being persecuted for reasons of race, religion, nationality, membership of a particular social group or political opinion, is outside the country of his nationality and is unable or, owing to such fear, is unwilling to avail himself of the protection of that country; or who, not having a nationality and being outside the country of his former habitual residence as a result of such events, is unable or, owing to such fear, is unwilling to return to it."[1] The Geneva Convention supplements the 1948 Universal Declaration of Human Rights which grants all human beings the right to flee their state. Both the international agreements mandate every state to respect this law and protect those who are seeking protection and not to send back refugees to their troubled home. While on humanitarian grounds, the conventions are laudable. But it is the practicality which has marred its effects. Not all refugees are demarcated from migrants and not all are regularized legally. Those refugees who are not registered, remain as illegal immigrants with no state.

Refugees and giving them asylum has also been a toy in the hands of those in power. During the Cold War, many migrants as refugees from Laos, Cambodia, and Vietnam were readily given refugee status in the Western Europe and America because they were victims of communism. The grant of asylum brings attention to the persecutor state, and in this case the USSR turned the situation into a political battle between the two power blocs.

In the current context, migrants and refugees are considered as intruders because they disturb the order of the state and its demographic structure. Recently, Germany showed its attitude towards refugees coming by crossing the

1. Article 1 (1) Convention Governing the Specific Aspects of Refugee Problems in Africa (Adopted on 10 September 1969 by the Assembly of Heads of State and Government. CAB/LEG/24.3.

sea to Greece and gathered international criticism. In response, Angela Dorothea Merkel, the Chancellor of Germany, announced welcoming of 800,000 refugees into Germany. However, Germany has not been alone in refusing to share the burden, there have been other European states and many outside Europe who do not want to cater to the non-nationals coming for refuge.

One of the reasons for this is that migrants when enter, work, and begin to reside in the new state, the locals start to protest them. The widely held opinion is that the non-nationals will take over their jobs. Back in 1851, French workforce comprised of Germans, Spaniards, Belgians and Swiss. In the1880s, Italians were working as miners, steelmakers and laborer in France. By 1960s, Spaniards were filled in agricultural and domestic service. And, Portuguese in 1970 were employed in the construction field, housekeeping and agriculture.

Secondly, the issue of racism is common and inhibits welcoming of non-nationals. The Bangladeshi people have been stateless and refugees for years. They were neither allowed in Pakistan after independence in 1971 nor welcomed in the neighboring state called Myanmar who does not wish its nationality to dilute. Migrant Bangladeshi people are known as Rohingya and they have no status or legal registration as refugees. Similar is the case with the stateless Biharis residing in pockets of Bangladesh. People originally part of pre-partition India's state called Bihar, the Muslim Biharis left after India's independence and entered Bangladesh. But after Bangladesh's independence, they were neither taken into Pakistan nor accepted in Bangladesh because Biharis supported Pakistan army and so were labeled as traitors.

Migrants and refugees who are given a status also demand rights and privileges. One such incident happened in France. France, eager to make its nationality accessible and make its national laws open, developed policies that encouraged "Progressive Inclusion" or integration of the foreigners. What happen later in 1975 as a result was that the non-nationals who were provided social rights started making their presence felt with demands for prayer rooms in workplace, hostels and public areas. Muslims wanted some dedicated bookshops, clothes shop, halal meat shops, etc. Recently, France made its policies stringent on the matter of "visibility of Islam" and by 2004 rolled out policies that prohibited expression of religious affiliations. So, the headscarf was banned from schools and other public areas. In 2007 and 2012 the migration policies were tightened further leading to series of riots and fights against discrimination by the human rights associations against the police.

Therefore, identity plays a key security role for migrants in the host state. Muslims in France face the issue of multiple allegiances because of their identity is distinct from the French people. They jostle with "social cohesion" that reminds them of the social contract that immigrants agreed decades earlier in France. On the other hand, France cannot be hostile towards the Islamic religion and is keen to maintain good relations with the Arab World. Citizenship, as a result, was required to evolve. France separated nationality from citizenship, meaning, that one could politically participate and yet be not national. Not just in France but multi-citizenship is now common in Germany, Canada, USA, UK and Portugal. However, it raises questions like who citizens are, non-nationals, nationals, non-national residents, non-national non-residents and refugees. Even if migrants become nationals of a state through papers, they continue to be different from true nationals. And, this marks the divide between identities and threatens the whole identity of a state. It has also transformed states and sovereignty.

Another challenge that a state faces because of migration is that from where nationals have left, a shortage of economic strength takes place, just as the famous "brain drain" happened when highly qualified youth chose to work in the developed parts of the North like USA, United Kingdom, Germany, France, etc. Malawi which should have more Malawian doctors and caregivers is deprived of their assistance because Manchester has more of the Malawian medical experts. However, this trend turned the issue of migrations as a profitable commodity for the host state because they now have begun to generate wealth and migration came to be associated with economic and political development. People who migrated to developed states, send funds to their families and in this way contribute to human development through remittances far more than official assistance. The Philippines, for instance, is dependent upon such transfers from the women who work in USA, Italy, Japan and Gulf states as migrant caregivers. China has over 50 million nationals living as migrants in other parts of the world and generating development funds for China. India is one of the most important states as a remittance receiving and sending state in the world. And, for all the South Asian states, remittances play a significant role for their economic development by easing their foreign exchange pressures and increase national savings, which is utilized for domestic investments. However, the challenge that the South Asian states face is the informal routes through which remittances enter their borders. Informal remittances not only mean that the remittances are largely undocumented but that the remittances have been generated through illegal activities like smuggling, money laundering, etc.

In addition, immigrant associations are formed which help the state of origin. Mexicans and Colombians have transnational organizations that partner with their state of origin and help in their nation's development. States like Mauritania, Senegal and Mali benefit from such associations and send regular funds for education, health, water supply, etc. This trend encourages the above-mentioned brain drain challenge for states and leads one to question whether states really want to resolve and control checks on migrations?

Migration is also a critical matter related to state security. Post 9/11 terrorist attacks, migration, terrorism and violence have shown an interconnection. Most of the terrorists involved in the attacks in USA, Paris, Madrid, etc. were either tourists or students. Signed in 1985, the Schengen Area raises questions on immigration and terrorism in Europe more than freedom of work and travel.

Conclusion

Migration is a global phenomenon and has transformative effects on a state and on the concept of citizenship. Migrations create an unavoidable change in the demographic structure, cultural values, and rights and privileges of the people. Therefore, while EU has provisions for its citizens that facilitate easy movement, EU also ensures that there are radars, drones and other monitoring systems that check the security levels of the borders and entry of illegal immigrants. Many states resort to bilateral agreements for framing policies on migrations, deportation and residence permit. Others resort to multilateral agreements that necessitate collective efforts.

Factors affecting migrations are search for a job and natural resources, political situation, transnational migrant networks, environmental factors, and increased urbanization. Challenges for the state are to prevent people to migrate and provide an assurance of well-being so that they are willing to reside, investment and trust their home state. There have been events when states have resorted to certain measures and ambitions to preserve the ties of the nationals and bring them back. Italians who left Italy were coddled by the Berlusconi Government hoping that it will provide votes in favor. Others have granted political and social rights for those nationals who fled.

The answer is in the state to rectify its developmental policies, become a stable democratic polity, expand economically, and reconsider its migration policies. A popular opinion in the 1980s for preventing nationals of Italy, Greece, Portugal and Spain from migrating to developed states of EU was by reforming the state politically and ending the dictatorship. However, not always development is the answer to solving the problem of migrations. Many times, migrations are generated because a state is developing and met an economic boom. Areas of the world which meet high standards or indices of human development are also the areas where people would naturally prefer to reside and invest for their future.

We are living in the era of global citizenship, transnational movement and trade, and cosmopolitan citizenship. Philosophers like Zygmunt Bauman talks about "liquid citizenship" wherein the raising borders and barriers will work against the evolution towards progress (Bauman 1993, 2000, 2005). Kofi Annan proposed in 2006 a Global Migration Group that would promote international and regional instruments on migrations. Such efforts set the stage for a multilateral approach to govern migration. Especially since most of the states are now places where several communities exist, and recognition of multiculturalism is a necessity. States are under a humanitarian obligation as well to provide refugee to stateless and environmentally displace people.

Yet, the whole issue of state and its borders is controversial as it is related to identity and the existence of a state. Borders define the area within which control is permissible. Borders help segregate one political entity from another. Places where borders are blur, the people there do not know which area they belong to and whether they are intruders or nationals. Importance of borders can be studied from the empires and the walls they created like the Great Wall of China and the Hadrian's Wall by Roman Empire. However, most importantly borders are crucial because they set an order of a state.

Being constantly evolving in nature, the value of borders and its political and economic articulations has been changing with time. As an international issue, migrations challenge the management of people and state in a diverse manner. It is a challenge to bring all the states, civil societies, churches, human rights organizations, organizations promoting migrants and refugees under a convention and discuss the goal and interests in a way that a hierarchy of interests is abolished. Even today, it is a slow process to broach the idea of conducting a global conference on migrations. Yet, one must not overlook the freedom of human beings and freedom of movement. Also, there is chaos between organizations regarding migrations and the responsibilities. The contradiction that it creates is something to reconcile with.

References

Balibar, Etienne (2002), *Politics and the Other Scene*, New York: Verso.

Balibar, Etienne (2004), *We, the People of Europe? Reflections on Transnational Citizenship*, Oxford: Princeton University Press.

Bauman, Zygmunt (1993), *Postmodern Ethics*, Oxford: Blackwell Publishers.

Bauman, Zygmunt (2000), *Liquid Modernity*, Cambridge: Polity Press.

Bauman, Zygmunt (2005), *Liquid Life*, Cambridge: Polity Press.

Bhagwati, J. N. (1976), *The Brain Drain and Taxation: Theory and Empirical Analysis*, Amsterdam: North-Holland.

Bhagwati, J. N. (1979), International Factor Movements and National Advantage", *Indian Economic Review* N. S., 14: 73-100.

Bhagwati, J. N. and K. Hamada (1974), "The Brain Drain, International Integration of Markets for Professionals and Unemployment: A Theoretical Analysis, *Journal of Development Economics*, I: 19-24.

Sharma, S. and D. Thapa (2013), Taken for Granted: Nepali Migration to India. Research Paper III, Centre for the Study of Labour and Mobility (CESLAM), Kathmandu, Nepal.

United Nations Population Division (2001), *Replacement Migration: Is it a Solution to Declining and Ageing Populations?*, New York: United Nations.

Chapter Eleven

Climate Change Induced Migration in Bangladesh

Priyanshi Chauhan

Abstract

Migration is a social phenomenon which can occur due to social and economic reasons. Bangladesh is one of the most vulnerable countries in the context of climate change. It is because of its sensitive ecology making it prone to floods, cyclones, tidal surges and bearing the effects of climate change which includes increasing salinity of rivers, soil salinity and increasing risk of submergence of land. Thus, climate induced migration has appeared as a new phenomenon in Bangladesh. Migration due to climate change can be within the country or outside the country. This paper attempts to comprehend the way in which the phenomenon of climate change induces migration by linking climate change with human displacement in Bangladesh. Different combinations of push and pull factors including the income of the individual access to resources and economic opportunities at home, and availability and demand of resources at the place of destination, wage structure of the destinaion and social linkages between the place of origin and destination has been explored. Also, this paper attempts to look at the socioeconomic changes that accompany the phenomenon of climate change migration in Bangladesh. Lastly, this paper analyses existing international legal framework and government policies to deal with the issue of climate migration.

Introduction

The climate of the earth has always been changing. However, the unprecedented pace with which it has changed in the recent past and the human contribution to climate change is a cause of worry. As reported by The Guardian in August 2016, National Aeronautics and Space Administration (NASA) announced that the earth is warming at a pace not seen in at least the past 1,000 years. The Industrial

Revolution, which replaced human labor with the machine and used coal as the primary fuel to run industries, marked a turning point in the earth's ecology and human-environment relationship.

Climate change is a complex phenomenon. Though it is environmental in nature it has consequences for all spheres of human existence including the social, political and economic. One such consequence of climate change is migration. This paper attempts to study the relationship between climate change and migration and identify various push and pull factors that influence the decision to migrate. It seeks to identify the drivers of migration in the case of climate change. The paper then uses these concepts to look at the various issues of climate change induced migration with a particular focus on socioeconomic dimensions. The last section of the paper looks at the existing provisions in the international law and the policies adopted by the Bangladesh government for climate change induced migration. The paper concludes that a comprehensive international framework and national policies are needed to address the challenges of climate change on population that are forced to migrate and migration should be seen as a possible adaptive strategy.

Theoretical Framework

As stated before, climate change is a complex phenomenon because the phenomenon is predominantly environmental but influences a whole range of activities in the social, political and economic spheres. One of the consequences of climate change is migration. Climate change makes certain inhabited areas on earth unviable to live. Therefore, people look for places where it is possible to survive and earn a living without the threat of destruction by extreme weather phenomenon and climate changes. However, climate change does not directly cause migration. This is where the multidimensionality of climate change comes in; the decision to migrate due to changes in climate is highly subjective and depends on various push and pull factors. Push factors are at the place of origin which makes conditions unviable and expensive to continue living there; pull factors are the incentives and conditions at the place of destination which attracts migrants and by reducing costs of migration and providing opportunities to earn a livelihood. As Anwer (2012) puts it,

> "The push factors are related to the place of origin including lack of economic opportunities, and lack of access to resources; the pull factors relate to the place of destination, including availability of employment and demand for workers,

> higher wages, political stability or access to resources. Thus according to push and pull theory of migration factors that facilitate or restrict migration include family or social networks, government policies, economic ties as well as social and cultural exchanges."

Brown (2008) in his paper Climate and Migration prepared for the International Organisation for Migration (IOM) states that,

> "Migration, even forced migration, is not usually just a product of an environmental "push" from a climate process like sea level rise. Except in cases of climate events, where people flee for their lives, it does require some kind of "pull": be it environmental, social or economic. There has to be the hope of a better life elsewhere, however much of a gamble it might be."

This means that the push and pull factors considered together with the push factor of the environmental phenomenon makes climate change induced migration a multi-causal phenomenon. Thus, relationship between climate change and migration cannot be studied without taking into account socioeconomic factors.

The categorisation of drivers of migration can be climatic factors and non-climatic factors. Climatic factors can be further categorised as climate processes and climate events. Climate processes are the changes in the climate which take place slowly over a due course of time. Rise in the sea level, salinisation of water, desertification, water scarcity, contamination of aquifers are few examples of climate processes. On the other hand, climate events are sudden hazards, for example floods, cyclones, storms, etc. This may cause sudden mass movements but generally of temporary nature. This is because such migration is caused by erratic weather behaviour and normalcy may return after it is over, making return possible. In case of climatic processes, migration is not sudden but generally of a permanent nature because the damage is permanent. Non-climatic factors, as the name suggests are those other than the environmental factors; for example source of income, wealth, and social links in the place of destination, government policies and adaptive strategies among others. The non-climatic factors are relatively predominant where migration is due to climatic processes as compared to climatic events. In the case of climatic events, surviving through the event is the main concern and people flee for life.

Neither Climate change will affect all people in the same manner, nor will its consequences be spread evenly. Thus, the decision to migrate as a response to climate change phenomenon will vary across countries, communities and social groupings. Walsham (2010) suggests that the consequences of climate change including its effects on migration will be most severe for developing countries. It has identified particular areas -including the Asian mega deltas -facing greater exposure and sensitivity to climate change combined with limited adaptive capacity to suggest that impacts will be most significant. Developing countries are the ones which have historically contributed the least to the climate changes and still will be the ones that will suffer the most severe consequences of it. Also, different social groups have different capacity for adaptation. Take the case of gender being a source of distinction for effect of climate change. Women are the historically deprived section of population that have limited access to public and private goods, participation in decision making, opportunities to earn and mobility. The social and economic constraints facing women put them at a disadvantage when adaptive strategies to deal with climate change are to be used. The UN Women Watch (2009) explains this in the following manner,

> "Women are more vulnerable to climate change as compared to men -primarily as they constitute the majority of world's poor and are more dependent on their livelihood on natural resources that are threatened by climate change. Furthermore, they face social, economic and political barriers that limit their coping capacities. Women and men in rural areas in developing countries are especially vulnerable when they are highly dependent on local natural resources for their livelihood. Those charged with the responsibility to secure water, food and fuel for cooking and heating face the greatest challenges. Second, when coupled with unequal access to resources and to decision making process, limited mobility places women in rural areas in a position where they are disproportionately affected by climate change. It is thus important to identify gender-sensitive strategies to respond to environmental and humanitarian crisis caused by climate change."

Thus, climate change induced migration should be understood with the whole range of social and economic factors along with the environmental phenomenon. As Brown (2008) puts it,

> "It must be recognised that degradation of the environment is socially and spatially constructed; only through a structural understanding of the environment in the broader political and cultural context of a region or country can one begin to understand the role it plays as a factor in population movement."

The Case of Bangladesh

Bangladesh has a unique geography which makes it particularly prone to climatic changes and processes. Bangladesh is a low lying country with two-thirds of its land area less than 5 metres above the sea level. These areas are vulnerable to tidal flooding, cyclones and related storm surges. The country is situated at the deltas of large rivers flowing from the Himalayas - the Ganges, the Brahmaputra and Meghna which exposes it to a range of flood and rain hazards. The country is also a global hotspot for tropical cyclones.

There is growing evidence of increasing environmental migration in Bangladesh. Walsham (2010) report for the IOM states that, "Bangladesh is already experiencing the growing phenomenon of environmental migration, with rural-urban migration increasing manifold leading to rapid and unplanned urbanisation in city centres such as Dhaka." According to IUCN (2015), about 15 million people in Bangladesh alone could be on the move because of climate change causing the worst migration in human history. The Bangladesh Climate Change and Action Plan (2009) states that, "It has been estimated that there is impending threat of displacement of more than 20 million people in the event of sea level change and resulting increase in salinity coupled with impact of increase in cyclones and storm surges, in the near future." A report by Displacement Solutions (2012), an organization that works with climate displaced persons, communities, governments and the UN to find a right based solutions to climate change, also states, "It is estimated that six million people have already been displaced by the effects of climate hazards in Bangladesh." All this suggest that the dangers of climate change and its impact on migration for the people of Bangladesh are real. While some have already become the victims of climate change, others are likely to suffer in the near future.

Shamsuddoha et.al (2012) explored that drought, monsoon floods, river erosion, saline water intrusion and tropical cyclones are the disasters that account for large scale displacement of people while erratic rainfall, excess rainfall, dense fog and storm and hail having little or insignificant impact on displacement in Bangladesh. The disaster events that initiate large scale migration are those which take away source of livelihood or makes people homeless or both. For instance, saline water intrusion makes the land unfit for agricultural production and also causes freshwater scarcity. These effects are of permanent nature. Monsoon floods, which are not uncommon in Bangladesh, makes people landless, homeless, damages crops and seed beds making people jobless. On the other hand, environmental phenomena that have little impact on migration are the ones which may have same type of impacts but the intensity and duration is much less. The push and pull factor that work here need to be understood. Recurrences of natural disasters, which undermine agricultural development and cause food crisis encourage people to live their homes. By contrast, the main factor that attracts them to urban centres is the expansion of non-agricultural sectors -industry and services, which promises jobs and higher household incomes (Anwer 2012). Sometimes, it is just one or two members of the family, generally male who decide to migrate in search of non-agricultural jobs leaving their families behind. The strategy here is to look for better incentives for livelihood while using agriculture to get income whenever conditions are fit for agriculture.

According to the World Bank, Bangladesh has experienced fast GDP growth rate of 7.1 percent in 2016. Despite this enormous growth rate many people continue to live in abject poverty in Bangladesh. According to the Asian Development Bank's Basic 2017 Statistics, 31.5 percent of population in Bangladesh is living below the national poverty line. This is the highest share of population below national poverty line when compared to other South Asian countries. The 2016 Human Development Report puts Bangladesh in the countries of medium human development with the rank of 139 out of 188 countries. Bangladesh is also one of the most densely populated countries in the world with World Bank reporting population density to be 1237 people per square km of land area in 2015. It is imperative to put this data in the analysis because it gives an idea about the nature of exposure of the people of Bangladesh to climate change and their vulnerability. The country is the hotspot for climatic events. But what makes it more vulnerable is not only the exposure to hazards but the possibility of it becoming a huge disaster because of poor adaptive capacities. The high poverty rate is significant because it forces people to live in the economically fragile and remote areas which are not preferred by the wealthier section of the society. Increasing population and high population density means that a large population is exposed to the risks of climate change and are therefore more vulnerable. Also, high population and population density put greater pressure on the environment as more people will compete for limited resources; for instance access to safe drinking water.

Agriculture is the main occupation of the people in Bangladesh. According to the World Bank, 47.78 percent of employed population is in the agricultural sector. The impact of climatic changes in Bangladesh will include rising temperatures and changing rainfall patterns, increased flooding, rising salinity in the coastal belts and droughts which are likely to reduce crop yields and crop production. This will lead to compromise on food security and people would migrate to look for livelihood and employment opportunities (Bangladesh Climate Change Strategy and Action Plan 2009).

Though, Bangladesh is a predominantly agrarian country it is experiencing urbanisation rate of 3.3 percent as of 2016 as stated by the World Bank. The environmentally vulnerable population in Bangladesh finds its new home in the urban slums bringing along with it a variety of problems like poor sanitation, overcrowding, prevalence of communicable diseases, unsafe drinking water, poverty and law and order problems among others.

Associated with this is the aspect of human security. Human security re-conceptualises security by moving away from traditional state-centric security to focus on individual. According to the United Nations Trust Fund for Human Security, "It brings together human elements of security, rights and development. It includes elements of economic security, food security, health security, environmental security, personal security, community security and political security." Climate induced migration makes people suffer from health and food insecurity. Also, not being able to find a livelihood some of them might face exploitation from trafficking, harassment by landlords, physical abuse, prostitution and violence. Others who may find a source of income for themselves may face exploitative terms of employment, for instance excessively long working hours or unpaid overtime work.

Also, mass migration can change the ethnic map of many countries and may cause political and ethnic tensions. In the case of Bangladesh, the Chittagong Hill Tracts are an attractive destination for migrants. The original inhabitants of CHT region are the non-Bengali hill tribes. The movement of Bengalis in the CHT region has caused ethnic tensions there. Also, India remains lucrative option for Bangladeshis to migrate due to cultural affinities and social network. The issue of illegal migration from Bangladesh in India is has caused tensions in the two countries and is a source of conflict in Indian states, especially Assam.

The Weather Channel (2017) reported that the Mora cyclone destroyed about 20,000 homes in the Cox Bazar region; 8000 residents were evacuated to storm shelters and hotels. Some 30,000 people were moved to more than 1000 shelters set up for evacuees in more than 10 districts most at risk by cyclone. Rohingya refugees a minority, was severely affected when their homes and camps were destroyed. Rohingyas are a stateless Muslim minority that face persecution and harassment in Myanmar. Many of them have migrated to Bangladesh to escape persecution. *The Time* (2017) reported that the BDRCS states that refugees were not among the evacuees because the locations where the encampments lie were not affected. However, Rohingya Community leader stated that their camps were not in the open and were now in the open air. This reaffirms the fact that a disadvantaged social group is more vulnerable to climatic changes. The Rohingyas in Bangladesh have no socio-political rights and are economically poor. They live in makeshift rehabilitation camps which were destroyed by strong winds. *Al Jazeera* (2017) reported that these refugees knew that there is a cyclone approaching but had nowhere to go. This highlights the fact that the refugee population which is stateless and is at a socioeconomic disadvantage are more vulnerable to the changes in climate change. Thus, the push and pull factors worked together and they are still living in the same area.

International Legal Framework and Policy Response in Bangladesh

While climate change induced migration is a reality, the international interest in resolving the crisis is limited. Even the terms and concepts referring to those who get displaced by climate change are not clear. The term 'environmental refugees' was coined by Lester Brown of the World Watch Institute (Boano, Zetter and Morris 2008) The UNEP termed these migrants as 'environmental refugees' -people who have been forced to leave their traditional habitat, temporarily or permanently, because of marked environment disruption (natural and/or triggered by people) that jeopardise their existence and/or seriously affect the quality of their life (Shamsuddoha and Chowdhury 2009). The term refugee, though depicts seriousness of the issue, it relies on the fact that people cross the international border and fails to consider those who get internally displaced due to climate change. Also, the term refugee is already in use in the international law defined in the 1951 Refugee Convention. Therefore, the term environmental or climate refugees have no legal basis and should be avoided. So, avoiding the term 'refugee', UNHCR has cautiously moved towards a definition of environmentally displaced persons as those: who are displaced from or who feel obliged to leave their usual place of residence, because their lives, livelihoods and welfare have been placed at serious risk as a result of adverse environmental, ecological or climatic processes and events (Boano, Zetter and Morris 2008). However, placing these persons into a category equivalent of Internally Displaced Persons (IDPs) reduces the burden on the international communities and makes national governments more responsible. But it must be recognised that climate change is a global phenomenon, dating back to the Industrial Revolution and it is the developing countries that are more affected by climate change. Developed countries bear historical responsibility towards it. So putting the burden on poor countries to face the crisis on their own is wrong. The term "climate evacuees" implies temporary movement within national borders. "Climate migrants" implies the "pull" of the destination more than the "push" of the source country and carries negative connotations which reduce the implied responsibility of the international community for their welfare (Brown 2008). Given the intensity of climate crisis in all parts of the world and the fact that the problem has arisen out of a global phenomenon, the people displaced due to climate change are in urgent need of recognition. Also many scholars suggest that recognition of displaced persons due to climate change will undermine many rights like Universal Declaration of Human Rights, Right to Adequate Housing and the right to self-determination. Shamsuddoha and Chowdhury (2009) write,

> "The 1948 Universal Declaration of Human Rights protects freedom of movements and social, cultural and economic rights which might be threatened when people are forced to migrate by climate induced environmental degradation."

They further state,

> "Observed and projected climate change will affect the right to adequate housing in several ways, i) sea level rise and storm surge will have a direct impact on the coastal settlements, ii) in the low-laying countries such impacts have already led to the relocation of people and communities, iii) settlements in low-laying mega deltas are also particularly at risk, as evidenced by the millions of people and homes affected by flooding and river erosion. All these will cause permanent displacement of people the people from their settlements to other areas."

Anwer (2012) writes,

> "The right to adequate housing is a basic human right under the International Covenant on Economic, Social and Cultural Rights as an element of an adequate standard of living. Observed and projected climate change will affect the right to adequate housing by sudden and slow onset disasters that influence permanent displacement from the areas of origin to the areas of destination."

Bangladesh in particular has National Environment Management Action Plan (1995) and Bangladesh Capacity Action Development Plan for Sustainable Environmental Governance (2007). The focus of these policies is addressing the various environmental challenges and little focus is on climate change induced migration. The Bangladesh Capacity Action Development Plan for Sustainable Environment Governance (2007) identifies the issue of displacement of human population due to river bank erosion and its social impact. It states,

> "It is estimated that more than 100,000 people are displaced annually due to river bank erosion. This results in devastating social impact along the major rivers. For example, poverty, woman and child trafficking, imbalance in social fabrics, in addition to productive land loss and enormous sediment yield are the major consequences of river erosion."

Despite acknowledging the problem, this is not followed by any action plan to address the problems that these migrants face. All of these documents are understandably focussed on meeting Bangladesh's current environment challenges and make few specific references to the migration effects of environmental challenges and make few specific references to the migration effects of environmental challenges and degradation (Walsham 2010). Other two important documents regarding climate change are the National Adaptation Plan of Action (2005) and Climate Change Strategy and Action Plan (2009). NAPA looks at the climate change induced migration in negative light and focuses on combating such migration. It thus overlooks migration as an effective adaptive strategy against climate change. The BCCSAP, however, goes a step ahead and identifies the threats of climate change and sees migration as a possible strategy of adaptation to address the effect of climate change. According to BCCSAP,

> "It has been estimated that there is impending threat of displacement of more than 20 million people in the event of sea level change and resulting increase in salinity coupled with impact of increase in cyclones and storm surges, in the near future. The settlement of these environmental refugees will pose a serious problem for the densely populated Bangladesh and migration must be

> considered as a valid option for the country. Preparation in the meantime will be made to convert this population into trained and useful citizens for any country."

However, despite these encouraging signs within more recent policy on climate change, it is fair to say that at present migration issues are not effectively mainstreamed with environmental, disaster management or climate change policy. Further, where migration is referenced, the tendency to concentrate on its negative dimensions -such as forced displacement or migration as a 'failure of adaptation' -is a barrier to introducing more proactive policy measure that maximise the benefits of migration from and between environmentally vulnerable regions (Walsham 2010). Migration is not only a manifestation of vulnerability of different social groups but should be seen as a coherent adaptive strategy. Traditionally, migration has been perceived as a major challenge that needs to be addressed. However, new studies suggest that migration can be seen as an effective adaptation strategy. The argument is that migration tends to reduce the impacts of environmental shocks and stresses and thus offset the vulnerability of the households to the impact of climate change. People may migrate individually, as a family or part of family, or as a community. Those who migrate individually or part of family send remittances back to family which may be used to support the community back home and boost their adaptive capacities. (Martin, et.al. 2013)

Conclusion

The threats that climate change poses to human race are real. The phenomenon of climate change induced migration affects people across social, economic and political dimensions. Adaptive strategies that countries need to undertake for mitigating the crisis should involve these socioeconomic dimensions. The human security concerns related to environmental migration need to be explored. This means that this phenomenon has to be managed by involving a combination of measures focussing on the vulnerability across different sections of people, risk reduction in the area of origin, planned urbanisation and settlement in the area of destination and ensure adequate aid and assistance to affected people and communities. The existing policy measures in Bangladesh highlight the ill effects of migration and aim to curb this migration as a solution to it. However, it must be realised that migration can be used as an effective adaptive strategy and for diversification of livelihood, and if planned and organised could facilitate in preventing the adverse effects of climate change on human population. For this, planning should involve the skill development of people to make them an asset for any country or city in case of migration. Also, community level adaptation involving local participation should be encouraged. At the international front, the developed countries should take the responsibility of the adverse effects of climate change. As stated before, climate change is a global phenomenon with local effects with different impacts on different countries and individuals. It is therefore not correct for developing countries, which are often ill-equipped to deal with such issues on their own both financially and technologically, to bear the burden by themselves when the now developed countries are bigger contributors to climate change. The first step should be to give recognition to those who are displaced due to climate change both internally and those who cross the international border and then create legal provisions to help those affected. This should involve equal participation from developing countries. It should also be realised that some areas on earth will become more viable and be better able to sustain larger populations due to climate change. For instance, higher temperatures are likely to extend growing seasons and reduce frost risk in mid to high-latitude areas. Erratic rainfall may increase rainfall in previously water-scarce regions. Thus, these pull factors of environment should be carefully studied and considered during policy making in the event of mass-migration due to climate change. Lastly, all the stakeholders -international communities, national government, vulnerable communities, civil society organisations and NGOs, private sector and the country's development partners among others should be identified and involved in the decision making.

References

Anwer, S. (2012). Climate Refugees in Bangladesh -Brotfür die Welt Retrieved 20 May , 2017, from https://www.brot-fuer-die-welt.de/fileadmin/mediapool/2_Downloads/Fachinformationen/Analyse/analyse_30_englisch_climate_refugees_in_Bangladesh.pdf.

Bangladesh Capacity Action Development Plan for Sustainable Environment Governance (Rep.). (2007). Dhaka, Bangladesh: Ministry of Environment and Forests, Government of the People's Republic of Bangladesh. doi:https://cmsdata.iucn.org/downloads/ncsa_compressed.pdf.

Bangladesh Climate Change Strategy and Action Plan 2009 (Rep.). (2009). Dhaka, Bangladesh: Ministry of Environment and Forests, Government of the People's

Republic of Bangladesh. doi:https://www.iucn.org/downloads/bangladesh_climate_change_strategy_and_action_plan_2009.pdf.

Basic 2017 Statistics -Economic Research and Regional Cooperation Department (Publication). (2017). Manila, Philippines: Asian Development Bank. doi:https://www.adb.org/sites/default/files/publication/298061/basic-statistics-2017.pdf.

Boano, C., Zetter, R., & Morris, T. (2008). Environmentally Displaced People: Understanding the Linkages between Environmental Change, Livelihoods and Forced migration (Policy brief No. 1). University of Oxford. doi:https://www.rsc.ox.ac.uk/files/files-1/pb1-environmentally-displaced-people-2008.pdf.

Brown, O. (2008). Migration and Climate Change (IOM Migration Series, Rep. No. 31). Geneva, Switzerland: International Organisation for Migration. doi:https://www.iom.cz/files/Migration_and_Climate_Change_-_IOM_Migration_Research_Series_No_31.pdf.

Chaney, E., & Wright, P. (30 May 2017). Tropical Cyclone Mora Makes Landfall in Bangladesh; 3 Killed, Thousands of Homes Destroyed. https://Weather.com. Retrieved 11 July 2017, from https://weather.com/news/weather/news/bangladesh-preps-impacts-tropical-cyclone-mora.

Climate Displacement in Bangladesh -The need for urgent housing, land and property (HLP) rights solutions (Rep.). (2012). Displacement Solutions.doi:http://ypsa.org/publications/DS%20-%20Climate%20Displacement%20in%20Bangladesh%20Report%20-%20May%202012.pdf.

Faruk, A. M. (2015, October 5). Climate Change Induced Migration in Bangladesh. International Union for Conservation of Nature. Retrieved 6 July 2017, from https://www.iucn.org/content/climate-change-induced-migration-bangladesh.

Human Development Report 2016 -Human Development for Everyone (Rep.). (2016). New York, New York: United Nations Development Programme. doi:http://hdr.undp.org/sites/default/files/2016_human_development_report.pdf.

Human Security In Theory And Practice. (n.d.). Retrieved 11 July 2017, from http://www.un.org/humansecurity/sites/www.un.org.humansecurity/files/human_security_in_theory_and_practice_english.pdf.

Martin, M., Kang, Y. H., Billah, M., Siddiqui, T., Black, R., &Kniveton, D. (2013). Policy analysis: Climate Change and Migration Bangladesh (Working paper No. 4). Dhaka, Bangladesh: RMMRU. doi:http://migratingoutofpoverty.dfid.gov.uk/files/file.php?name=wp4-ccrm-b-policy.pdf&site=354.

Milman, O. (2016, August 30). Nasa: Earth is warming at a pace 'unprecedented in 1,000 years'. Retrieved11 July 2017, The Guardian from https://www.theguardian.com/

environment/2016/aug/30/nasa-climate-change-warning-earth-temperature-warming.

National Adaptation Plan of Action Bangladesh (Rep.). (2005). Dhaka, Bangladesh: Ministry of Environment and Forests, Government of the People's Republic of Bangladesh. doi:https://unfccc.int/resource/docs/napa/ban01.pdf.

National Environment Management Action Plan (Rep.). (1995). Dhaka, Bangladesh: Ministry of Environment and Forests, Government of the People's Republic of Bangladesh. doi:http://documents.worldbank.org/curated/en/329001468741610744/pdf/multi-page.pdf.

Rohingya camps in Bangladesh destroyed by Cyclone Mora. (2017, June 1). Al Jazeera. Retrieved 11 July2017, from http://www.aljazeera.com/news/2017/05/cyclone-mora-adds-rohingya-plight-bangladesh-170531152048820.html.

Shamsuddoha, M., & Chowdhury, R. K. (2009, April). Climate Change Induced Forced Migrants: in need of dignified recognition under a new Protocol. Retrieved 11 July 2017, from http://www.glogov.org/images/doc/equitybd.pdf.

Shamsuddoha, Md, SM MunjurulHannan Khan, SajidRaihan and Tanjir Hossain (2012). Displacement and Migration from Climate Hot-spots: Causes and Consequences. Center for Participatory Research and Development and ActionAid Bangladesh, Dhaka: December, 2012.

Solomon, F. (31 May 2017). Thousands Displaced as Powerful Cyclone Hits Bangladesh, Prompting Fears for Rohingya Refugees. Time. Retrieved 11 July2017, from http://time.com/4799035/bangladesh-myanmar-cyclone-mora-rohingya/.

United Nations Women Watch.(2009). Women, Gender Equality and Climate Change [Fact sheet].Retrieved 25 May2017 from http://www.un.org/womenwatch/feature/climate_change/downloads/Women_and_Climate_Change_Factsheet.pdf.

Walsham, M. (2010). Assessing the Evidence :Environment, Climate Change and Migration in Bangladesh (Rep.). Geneva, Switzerland: International Organisation for Migration. doi:http://publications.iom.int/system/files/pdf/environment_climate_change_bangladesh.pdf.

Index

J